Rejoice Together

Rejoice Together

Prayers, Meditations
and Other Readings for Family,
Individual and Small Group Worship

Second Edition

EDITED BY
HELEN PICKETT

SKINNER HOUSE BOOKS
BOSTON

Printed in the USA.

Cover design by Kathryn Sky-Peck
Text design by Suzanne Morgan

ISBN 1-55896-495-9
978-1-55896-495-2

Library of Congress Cataloging-in-Publication Data
Rejoice together : prayers, meditations and other readings for family, individual,
and small group worship / edited by Helen Pickett.—2nd ed.
    p. cm.
  ISBN-13: 978-1-55896-495-2 (pbk. : alk. paper)
  ISBN-10: 1-55896-495-9 (pbk. : alk. paper)
  1. Unitarian Universalist Association—Liturgy—Texts. 2. Unitarian Universalist
Association—Prayer-books and devotions—English. I. Pickett, Helen (Helen R.)

BX9853.R45 2005
264'.09132—dc22

                        2005023218

9 8 7 6 5 4 3 2 1
08 07 06 05

Contents

Introduction

The word *worship* comes from the Middle English *worshipe*, which means worthiness. We worship, then, whenever we ascribe worth to some value, idea, object, person, experience, attitude, or activity, or whenever we give form or expression to that which we have already found to be of worth.

A worship experience can happen at any time, whether one is alone or part of a group. We worship when we take note of something beautiful; when we feel a deep sense of connectedness with other people, with the natural world, or with the transcendent (however defined); when we gain insight or a new sense of wholeness; when we struggle with an ethical challenge—whenever we deliberately focus our lives on something larger than ourselves.

Rejoice Together was first published in 1995 to help laypersons plan and conduct simple worship services or special ceremonies in family or small group settings. This new edition provides a broader and more contemporary selection of readings, collected primarily from Unitarian Universalist sources. Readings are arranged by the role they play in religious observance. Within these categories, such as "Opening Words" and "Table Graces," readings are further divided thematically to help you find easily those that will be most appropriate for your particular needs. May this collection enrich your time together as a family or small group coming together in common worship.

Helen Pickett
November 2005

Family Worship

Some two hundred years ago, when Unitarianism and Universalism were both new in North America, prayers were part of the typical family's daily ritual. Gradually we have let go of this practice. Though some UU families still say grace at meals or encourage children to say bedtime prayers, many have abandoned even these simple customs.

Some form of religious observance, whether you call it worship, celebration, or something else, is necessary to our spiritual growth whether we're part of a congregation or not. We may worship, celebrate, sing, and meditate by ourselves when we feel the need. We may also create opportunities to do these things together as families in our own homes.

Reverend Robert L'Hommedieu Miller, former member of the Church of the Larger Fellowship's Religious Education Committee, writes,

> The stuff of your daily life experience and its language and style of expression should provide content and context for family celebrations. Our celebrations affirm our beliefs in the goodness of life, the supreme worth of persons, the creative process of sharing, the search for truth. Our celebrations clarify our values and help us to learn what is good, what kind of person am I, what kind of persons are others? Our celebrations enhance our feeling of fellowship, oneness, awareness of traditions, family roots, and heritage, a sense of freedom to speak, think, and participate.

How can Unitarian Universalist families, especially those who do not live near a UU congregation, create their own occasions for religious observance? Here are some ideas and suggestions to stimulate your creativity.

Gather Around the Dinner Table

Try to find at least one time during the week when the whole family can sit down for a meal together. It may turn out to be a weekend breakfast instead of an evening meal. If you gather regularly around the table, you have more opportunities for the simple observances that can make time together meaningful for all. You can say grace together or share lines of poetry or other readings that are meaningful to you. Take turns saying grace in your own words, or hold hands around the table for a silent grace, passing around a hand-squeeze to say "Amen."

Light a Chalice or a Candle

You can make your own chalice by placing a small votive candle in a shallow bowl. When you sit down together, take turns lighting the chalice and saying special words. Or simply say,

> Today, I'm thankful for . . . .
> This flame is to help us remember . . . .
> Today, I'm thinking about . . . .
> This day is important to me because . . . .

Celebrate Birthdays and Seasonal Markers

Birthdays offer a great opportunity to celebrate individual members of your family or group. Take a few minutes to reflect on the past year and share favorite memories of the birthday person. Allow them to share their own memories as well. Reflect together on the ways in which that person has grown and their hopes for the coming year.

You can also honor the contributions of others by choosing a famous person's birthday to celebrate each month. Let various members of the family be responsible for decorations, food, and appropriate stories, readings, or songs. If a cake with candles makes it Happy Birthday time at your house, then do it for Thomas Jefferson and Clara Barton as well!

Create a Setting

Preparing a special place for your worship service affirms the importance of this time for your family and helps to set the tone. Here are some suggestions:

~ After eating, clear the table and place a chalice, candles, flowers, or special objects on it.

~ Form a half-circle of chairs around the fireplace, perhaps adding a special picture on the mantelpiece.

~ Spread a brightly colored cloth on the floor, arranging bits of nature or art around your chalice in the center. Sit around it in a circle.

~ Gather outdoors in a beautiful spot.

Create Services Together

Set up a box or paper bag in which you can drop ideas for services as they occur to you. Themes can be as diverse as P. T. Barnum's birthday, the Harvest Moon, helping others, making your home ecologically responsible, and Black History Month.

At the end of your family worship, while you are still gathered together, let someone reach into the box or bag and pull out a slip of paper with a theme. Decide as a group who is to be responsible for creating a visual focal point, opening words, a song, a reading, and a closing. Agree to present this service the next time you gather.

You might also plan a service around religious questions that members of the family raise. (Do we believe in Jesus? What happens when people die? Why do bad things happen?) Take some time to gather ideas and materials that focus on the question in different ways. Encourage other members of the family to say how they feel about the question. The point is not so much to answer the question as to give it the attention and importance that it deserves and to keep those big questions coming.

Designing a service in which the basic elements can be repeated from week to week establishes a comforting sense of familiarity and ritual. Here is how one family gathers every Sunday morning in their living room: Each member of the family lights a candle. Then someone reads opening words from this collection, a favorite poem, or something appropriate from a newspaper, magazine, or book. Recorded music is played. Each person shares their high points and low points of the past week, what they are looking forward to in the coming week, and anything they are worrying about. Someone volunteers to present information or background on the chosen theme of the service, as well as some thoughts and questions for discussion, as appropriate. At the end, someone reads closing words or the family sings together.

Group Worship

Unitarian Universalists gather for worship out of a desire for some kind of shared and worthwhile experience. A worship service is a deliberate shaping, ordering, or recalling of individual thoughts and experiences in the context of a community that shares common values, ideas, and attitudes.

The setting created by the worship leader or leaders is just as important as the content of any service. Many nonverbal dimensions of the worship experience can directly affect the quality of the service. Here are a number of suggestions to help you offer a rewarding worship experience for everyone involved.

Prepare for the Service

Spend some time identifying and focusing the theme of your service. Perhaps there is a seasonal holiday; an event of significance in the community; an ethical, political, or religious controversy; or a personal issue you wish to address. A clear focus is essential.

Make an outline of the components you envision in your service. With a general plan in mind, choose readings, meditations, music, and other elements that you feel enrich your theme.

Make copies of all of your selected materials and place them securely in an attractive binder or folder in the order in which you will present them.

When you have the whole service organized, read through it carefully. Note any special materials you may need to have on hand (candles, lighters, flowers) or people who must be asked to take part (pianist, ushers). Practice reading the service aloud at a slow, measured pace. People who are not trained as public speakers often speak much too quickly. Ask someone to listen and comment on your delivery.

Make a checklist of all the things that must be taken care of before the service begins. When you have tended to these details, you are ready! Take a deep breath and proceed.

Create a Setting

The worship area should be prepared so that it reflects the worth and beauty of what is being affirmed and celebrated. First impressions are important. Is the worship space clean, neat, and cared for? Is it bright and welcoming? Are the chairs and other furniture thoughtfully and pleasingly arranged? Is the lighting comfortable? (Sometimes softening the lighting just as the service begins is very effective.) The worship space should reflect the care and concern you have for your Unitarian Universalist faith.

Arranging the room to draw attention to a central point—perhaps next to the podium or pulpit—enhances the experience of comfort, community, inspiration, and common purpose that shared worship can offer. Simplicity is usually the key to effective use of flowers, paintings, sculptures, or banners. If possible, find an object that is related to the day's theme to provide symbolic reinforcement of the message. Symbols are particularly well suited to worship because they invite viewers to ponder their personal responses.

Live plants or flower arrangements can help to create an atmosphere of peace, reflection, and beauty. Place them carefully to complement other worship-space objects such as the chalice, symbols, or banners.

Create an Order of Service

A printed Order of Service helps participants relax because they know that they do not have to worry about being surprised or confused during the service. Even if the group regularly recites or sings something together, make sure the words are printed for visitors.

Start on Time

Beginning on time reduces the discomfort of visitors and communicates to everyone that you take the service seriously. Some UU groups use a gentle gong, a bell, or soft prelude music to let people know that the service is about to begin and that it is time for them to take their seats and prepare themselves for worship.

Light the Flame of Fellowship

The ritual lighting of a candle or chalice at the start of a service can become a powerful and meaningful symbol to focus group worship. You may do this with or without spoken words.

Include Music

Music can inspire religious and spiritual experiences that words cannot. Music evokes moods of celebration and contemplation, amplifying and complementing the spoken word. Live music has excitement and immediacy, but recorded music, if carefully selected and skillfully presented, can also be effective. Group singing invites active participation in the service.

Affirm Participation

Individuals who come to worship are participating merely by their presence. In addition, participation can be formalized by communal activities such as singing, unison and responsive readings, and affirmations; sharing announcements, personal joys, concerns, and prayers; and time for feedback after the service or questions and dialogue structured into the service. As a rule, some structured participation enriches worship, but services can be effective without it. Offering a variety of opportunities to participate can prevent staleness and encourage engagement in the service for all who attend.

Here are some additional resources for planning and conducting Unitarian Universalist worship, all available from the UUA Bookstore, 25 Beacon Street, Boston, MA 02108. You can also order online at **www.uua.org/bookstore**, or call 800-215-9076.

Great Occasions, edited by Carl Seaburg, Skinner House Books

Handbook of Religious Services, Church of the Larger Fellowship

One and Universal: Prayers and Meditations from Around the World, edited by John Midgley, Skinner House Books

Singing the Journey: A Supplement to Singing the Living Tradition, Unitarian Universalist Association

Singing the Living Tradition, Unitarian Universalist Association

You can also consult the UUA Worship Web at **www.uua.org/worshipweb**.

Opening Words

In This Sacred Place

Into this place may we come
    to share,
    to learn,
    to speak,
    to listen,
and to grow together in the spirit of peace and harmony
      and love.

FRANCES REECE DAY

Let us enter this place for the purpose of worship.
Here may our sorrows be comforted,
our inactions questioned,
our inquiry after truth continued,
our hearts uplifted,

our minds strengthened,
and ourselves stirred to greater achievements of good.

Here may our inner selves meet the Source of All Life.
This is a place of wonder and worship.

JAMES C. BREWER

Come in from the cold:
    Make yourself a religious home,
    if only for these brief moments—
    in spite of time,
    which shall soon bear us away from one another.
Make this a family.
Treat us as your own:
    Make us a religious family—
    if only in this space,
    which we make sacred
    by our connections here and beyond.
Come on in.
Make yourself at home.
Sing and love life.

ANDREW BACKUS

Welcome to this place of possibility!
This is love's hearth, the home of hope,
    a refuge for minds in search of truth unfolding, ever beautiful,
        ever strange.
Here, compassion is our shelter,
    freedom our protection from the storms of bigotry and hate.
In this place, may we find comfort and courage.
Here may our sight become vision to see the unseen,
    to glimpse the good that is yet to be.

MARIANNE HACHTEN COTTER

Welcome to this place.
Here we seek justice and truth.
Here we celebrate life and contemplate mystery.
Here we find healing and wholeness.
Welcome.

RAYMOND R. NASEMANN

Rejoice

Everybody wake up!
Open your eyes! Stand up!
Be children of the light—strong, swift, and sure of foot.
Hurry, clouds, from the four quarters of the universe.
Come, big snows, that water will be abundant this summer.
Come, ice, cover the fields, that the seeds may grow into good crops.
All hearts be glad!

PUEBLO SONG

These are the days that have been given to us;
    let us rejoice and be glad in them.
These are the days of our lives;
    let us live them well in love and service.
These are the days of mystery and wonder;
    let us cherish and celebrate them in gratitude together.
These are the days that have been given to us;
    let us make of them stories worth telling to those who come
        after us.

WILLIAM R. MURRY

Let there be joy in our coming together.
Let there be truth heard in the words we speak and the songs we sing.
Let there be help and healing for our disharmony and despair.
Let there be silence for the voice within us and beyond us.
Let there be joy in our coming together.

CARL SEABURG

Together

We come together now to worship.
Spirit calls to spirit.
Hand reaches out to hand.
Heart joins with heart.
Voice lifts with voice a song of praise.
Come, let us worship together.

CALVIN O. DAME

It is a blessing to be.
It is a blessing to be here.
It is a blessing to be here now.
It is a blessing to be here now, together.

ANONYMOUS

Our lives are made up of small moments:
    sharing a meal with friends or family,
    wondering about a question that puzzles us,
    giving help to another,
    listening to a person and being listened to,
    talking with another about something that makes us sad,
    an embrace, a smile, a touch,
    offering a thought that might help, just a little, to make
        more sense of it all.
Our gathering here is just such a small moment.
It is a small thing we do in gathering. Yet it is significant.
May we affirm and celebrate the moments that we share here today.

BRUCE MARSHALL

Children all,
We come together
In faith and hope,
To find what meaning life holds for us,
To laugh and sing with one another,
To soothe the wounds of daily life,
And to grow together in wisdom and love.

MARJORIE C. SKWIRE

In this time we turn our thoughts to how we can
    touch and be touched,
    love and be loved,
    forgive and be forgiven,
    heal and be healed,
so that the goodness of our lives is a shared blessing.

MARTA M. FLANAGAN

All that quickens sympathetic imaginings,
all that awakens sensitivity to others' feelings,
all that strengthens courage,
all that adds to the love of living—
belongs to us.
May our spirits be quickened and enriched, strengthened and
    enhanced by our being here together.

GEORGE G. BROOKS

Welcome
    to a day of hope and promise,
    to a place of peace and comfort,
    to a journey toward truth and justice,
    and to a community of love and courage
    that will help us along the way.

ANITA FARBER-ROBERTSON

Our UU Values

We have come together today,
not because we expect to find answers here,
but rather because we expect to be encouraged in our questioning.

We have come together today,
not because we expect to find perfect people here,
but rather because we hope to find authentic people here.

We have come together today,
not because we are certain of our own righteousness,
but because we are continually searching for the right, the good, the
    uplifting.

We have come together today,
not because we seek absolution for our sins and failures,
but rather because we acknowledge our imperfections and seek the
    courage
to make amends for those failures to ourselves and others.

We have come together today,
not because we need to be told what to believe and how to act,
but rather because we need each other's encouragement
to act according to our own best beliefs.

We have come together today,
not because we are hoping to find God in a scripture or a ritual,
but rather because we are hoping to discover the divinity
within our own hearts and within the hearts of others.

We have come together today,
not because we believe that holiness exists within these walls alone,
but rather to have our hearts and minds directed to the holiness in
    the world.

For all of these reasons, we have come together today.

SUZANNE MEYER

We are here as we are—
    mortal, concerned, life-affirming,
    turned toward joy, facing our woes—
to worship, to behold the mysteries of life and death
without shield of creed or comfortable credulity.

May our celebration, in word, silence, sign, and song,
help move us into the company of that great cloud of witnesses
    who lived to unveil ever-deeper truth,
    who yielded the wine of faithfulness
        when history's hard press was upon them,

who honed their lives, no less fragile or strong than our own,
on the whetstone of your demands and ecstasies, O love.
Life of our own lives, we begin again, intent on the good.

MARK BELLETINI

Many of the past generation and many today have found three
abiding values in prayer:
the quiet meditation on life,
the reaching out toward the universal and the infinite,
and the courageous facing of one's profoundest wishes.
Let parents sense and share with their children the glory and
mystery of everyday things.
Let them look with sympathy upon humanity's age-long dilemmas.
Let no questions be taboo.
The next generation can ill afford to have the deeper values deleted
from the book of life.

SOPHIA LYON FAHS

Understanding

We come together to celebrate who we are, to share the insights that
give meaning and hope to our lives, to learn from the wisdom
of others, that their truths may contribute to our understanding.
We gather, we share, we learn; we celebrate our coming together.

ANN PEART

We come from the ineffable One,
source and goal of all that is.
We create a self, separate and unique,
a window in the rosette of the soul
where divine light shines through
in a rainbow of colors.

At journey's end we discover
what we always knew to be true
but only dimly perceived:
We are one with the One
which alone truly is.

RICHARD FEWKES

We gather this day; we come in search of life's meaning.
All of us have moments of weakness and times of strength;
    all sing songs of sorrow and love.
May our worship bring us strength along our way.
In the presence of the sacred, may we come to know our true
    selves, finding a fresh impulse to love and do good.

MARTA M. FLANAGAN

We pause in reverence before the wonder of life,
    the wonder of this moment,
    the wonder of being together, so close yet so apart,
    each hidden in a secret chamber,
    each listening, each trying to speak,
    yet none fully understanding,
    none fully understood.

We pause in reverence before all intangible things
    that eyes see not, nor ears can detect,
    that hands can never touch,
    that space cannot hold,
    and time cannot measure.

Fling wide the windows, O my soul!
The bright beams of morning are warm.

SOPHIA LYON FAHS

We come together today seeking a reality beyond our narrow selves
that binds us in compassion, love, and understanding to other
human beings, and to the interdependent web of all living things.

May our hearts and minds be opened to the power and the
insight that weave together the scattered threads of our experience
and help us remember the Wholeness of which we are a part.

WAYNE B. ARNASON

Amid all the noise in our lives,
we take this moment to sit in silence—
    to give thanks for another day,
    to give thanks for all those in our lives who have brought us
        warmth and love,
    to give thanks for the gift of life.

Let us open ourselves, here, now,
to the process of becoming more whole—
    of living more fully,
    of giving and forgiving more freely,
    of understanding more completely the meaning of our lives
        here on this earth.

TIMOTHY D. HALEY

This hour is sacred because we make it so!
By our presence with each other we renew our bonds.
Let us join together in compassion and understanding to seek wisdom.
Let us turn aside from transient cares and contemplate anew the
enduring mystery that is life.
Let us open ourselves to receive the gifts of love and peace.

JIM WICKMAN

Welcome to this time of seeking and finding, for it is in our coming
together here that we celebrate who we are and who we yet shall be.

JANE ELLEN MAULDIN

Promise

A day,
yes, another day—
this day is ours:
its beauty, its promise,
its weight of sorrow and disappointment,
the brightness of its opportunity for doing and achieving,
of its opportunity for the deepening of love and understanding.
This day is ours, even as we make it ours

by the readiness and warmth of our appreciations,
for from it we shall receive according to the measure of our giving.
Let our giving be of ourselves, and from the heart.
May there be laughter in this day, and if there be tears, then
   generous tears.
Another day?
Ah, yes—a day.

VINCENT SILLIMAN

For untold centuries people have drawn apart from the workaday world to worship, to celebrate, and to wonder at things beyond and within themselves.

So we are gathered here to raise our sights and look at new horizons. Life is more than toil for bread; life has meaning and purpose.

As we celebrate life together, let us seek harmony within ourselves, with one another and the world, and find our lives uplifted and made whole.

MARYELL CLEARY

We summon ourselves from the demands and delights of the daily round
   from the dirty dishes and unwaxed floors,
   from unmowed grass and untrimmed bushes,
   from all incompletenesses and not-yet-startednesses,
   from the unholy and the unresolved.

We summon ourselves to attend to our vision
    of peace and justice,
    of cleanliness and health,
    of delight and devotion,
    of the lovely and the holy,
    of who we are and what we can do.

We summon the power of tradition and the exhilaration of newness,
    the wisdom of the ages and the knowing of the very young.
We summon beauty, eloquence, poetry, music to be the bearers of
    our dreams.

We would open our eyes,
    our ears,
    our minds,
    our hearts
to the amplest dimensions of life.

We rejoice in manifold promises and possibilities.

GORDON B. MCKEEMAN

Come, dear friends.
Come into this hour of worship and togetherness.
Come with eyes ready to see,
    a throat willing to sing,

ears open to hear,
a mind eager to know,
and a heart poised to feel.
Enter fully into this hour of worship and togetherness—and be blessed.

SCOTT W. ALEXANDER

Come, let us worship together.

Let us open our minds to the challenge of reason,
open our hearts to the healing of love,
open our lives to the calling of conscience,
open our souls to the comfort of joy.

Astonished by the miracle of life,
grateful for the gift of companionship,
confident in the power of living faith,
we are here gathered.

Come, let us worship together.

LINDSAY BATES

Stillness

May our souls be united in praise and wonder
for that which remains still amid the flow;
for that which remains quiet amid the music;
for that which remains cool amid the heat;
for that which remains dark amid the blaze;
for that which remains alive amid death;
for that which remains while all is changing.
For all these let us give thanks and praise.

W. FREDERICK WOODEN

We stop. We pause. We pay attention. We center ourselves.
We free ourselves from the compulsion of projects to finish,
    work to be done, things to accomplish.
We leave ourselves alone for a time.
We journey deep down into that quiet center where no voice is heard.
We live for a brief time on an island of peace.
We apprehend the world from a quiet center.
Here is the center of the world.
In this instant are centered the whirling orbs, the movement of earth
    and sky.

In this fragile moment of time is the culmination of all that has
been and the promise of all that shall be.
Here in our grasp, in this moment, is the center of the world.

RICHARD S. GILBERT

Loss

We pause this hour to remember
    those whom we have lost,
    those whom we fear losing,
    those from whom we are separated,
    those to whom we would extend a helping hand, a caring heart,
        the will to live.
We pause this hour also to hope
    for life and good living,
    for love and kind words,
    for reconciliation,
    for the support of family and friends,
    for meaning in our struggle,
    for wholeness.
May our memories and hope renew us for the days and nights to come.

M. SUSAN MILNOR

Seasonal and Special Occasions

Spring

Today we come, as people have come for thousands of years,
    to worship and sing praises,
    to celebrate the victory of hope over despair,
    to be reminded of the ever-renewing life of the spirit,
    and to mark the season of springtime come again.
Welcome to our festival of joy!

POLLY LELAND-MAYER

May we be united in praise and wonder.
Let us bless this moment that, though brief, is precious to eternity.
Let us bless the hour, that it is given us to shape and for us to be
    shaped by.
Let us bless the day, that it is new and yet familiar, fresh and yet venerable.
Let us bless the season, that it is fragrant with flowers and loud with
    insects.
Let us bless the power that pours forth moments, hours, days,
    weeks, months, years, in careless generosity, much as
    dandelions and mosquitoes spill out in May.

W. FREDERICK WOODEN

Summer

Let us rejoice in the light of this day,
in the glory and warmth of the summer sun, and
in the blooming and bursting of new life.
Let us rejoice in the earth with its grass and trees,
its weeds and flowers, its many fruits and hidden treasures.
Let us rejoice together this day.

CONNIE STERNBERG

Thanksgiving

We gather this morning in the spirit of thanksgiving:
    we give thanks for this family/fellowship,
    for the bounty of this season,
    for beauty of earth and sky, and of human creations,
    for love, given and received.
Let us make our thanks for these blessings manifest in our words
    and in the warmth of our companionship.
Let us say "thanks" to Life!

MARYELL CLEARY

Christmas

In the Spirit of Christmas Past,
let us gather to listen and learn
the ancient stories,

that our hearts may find wisdom.

In the Spirit of Christmas Present,
let us gather to view and question
the way things are,

that our hearts may seek justice.

In the Spirit of Christmas Future,
let us gather to dream and to plan
the way things will be,

that our hearts may be reclaimed by hope.

LAURALYN BELLAMY

Welcome, rich season of bounty and good cheer! Wreathe every life with garlands of innocent mirth. Crown with green wreaths of joy the brows of those we love; weave in red berries of health, and the bright star of hope.

Welcome, blest season of peace, that bringest a truce to strife! And may thy white wings of peace spread over the waiting earth. Link all peoples and nations in the sure bonds of community, shed peace and good will, good will and peace, on all humanity.

PERCIVAL CHUBB

We are the ones who keep Christmas. Christmas is what we want it to be. Christmas is loveliness, happiness, singing, laughter, giving, and sharing, if we will make it so.

May this season be a time of rebirth and renewal, a time of happiness and joy. Let there be light and warmth, and let us be their bearers.

JEANNE H. M. BELL

Chalice and Candle Lightings

Transformation

We light this chalice to affirm that new light is ever waiting to break through to enlighten our ways,

That new truth is ever waiting to break through
to illumine our minds,

And that new love is ever waiting to break through to warm our hearts.

May we be open to this light and to the rich possibilities that it brings us.

CHARLES HOWE

For every time we make a mistake
and we decide to start again,
    we light this chalice.

For every time we are lonely
and we let someone be our friend,
    we light this chalice.

For every time we are disappointed
and we choose to hope,
    we light this, our chalice.

M. MAUREEN KILLORAN

For centuries people have told stories, celebrated life, and
approached the ultimate while gathered around a fire.
Today we light this chalice
    that the hearth fire of our hearts may be rekindled,
    that our stories may be retold,
    that we might celebrate life anew, and
    that we might approach what is of ultimate value.

DENISE D. TRACY

We light this flame
this symbol of energy
of light, of life
to remind us
of the energy within us
of the light of our life
of the light that is in us
of the light that *is* us.

JANET GOODE

(*Extinguish the chalice*)

We now extinguish this flame
but not our energy.
We extinguish this flame
but not the light of our life.
We extinguish this flame
but not the light that *is* us.

JANET GOODE

We light this chalice for the light of truth.
We light this chalice for the warmth of love.
We light this chalice for the energy of action.

MARY ANN MOORE

The light of this chalice is a frail thing.
It can be snuffed out by the winds of cynicism and apathy.
May its little flame be a reminder of the power of the spirit.
Let us rededicate ourselves to providing light that lifts
　　our hearts and increases the world's joy.

ALAN G. DEALE

To face the world's coldness,
　　a chalice of warmth.
To face the world's terrors,
　　a chalice of courage.
To face the world's turmoil,
　　a chalice of peace.
May its glow fill our spirits, our hearts, and our lives.

LINDSAY BATES

May this light kindle within us
　　the warmth of compassion
　　the glow of love
　　the fire of commitment
　　the light of truth.

MARIANNE HACHTEN COTTER

In flame from this chalice
we find the light of faith,
the glow of hope,
and the warmth of service.
May we ever grow in faith, hope, and service
as we kindle our own lights from its spark.

WAYNE B. ARNASON

We light our flaming chalice
to illuminate the world we seek.
In the search for truth, may we be just;
in the search for justice, may we be loving;
and, in loving, may we find peace.

ELIZABETH MCMASTER

May the flame here lit
be to us a symbol of the torch
that is passed from hand to hand, and life to life—
of caring and concern and the passion for involvement
which have marked the men and women of our liberal faith
for many generations.

PHILIP R. GILES

This flame affirms the light of truth, the warmth of love, and the fire of commitment.

ELIZABETH SELLE JONES

(*Extinguish the chalice*)

We extinguish this flame but not the light of truth, the warmth of love, or the fire of commitment which it here symbolizes. These we carry in our hearts until we come together again.

ELIZABETH SELLE JONES

May the lighting of this flame renew in us our endless
        search for all that is right and true,
our abiding love of life and all who share this life,
and our unending dedication to following paths of peace
        and justice.

ELIZABETH B. STEVENS

As the polestar once guided explorers,
may the flame of this chalice guide us
to ever better understandings of
ourselves and our universe.

NORMAN V. NAYLOR

The Unifying Spirit

We light the flame of knowledge;
>   may understanding be with us.
We light the flame of love;
>   may caring be among us.
We light the flame of holiness;
>   may the unifying spirit be within us.

EDWIN LYNN

May unity and peace abide within us.
May wholeness and joy touch our hearts.
May kindness and compassion fill our universe
>   and reverence fill our days.
May we see the light that shines in all.

GARY KOWALSKI

May this flame be
>   as the light of wisdom in our minds
>   and as the warmth of love in our hearts.

HAROLD E. BABCOCK

Glory be to the earth and the wind.
Glory be to the sun and the rain.
Glory be to animals and children
　　and women and men.
Glory be to our holy flame
　　which calls us together as one.

BETTYE A. DOTY

Let the lighting of the chalice remind us that we can recognize the value of light only when we know, as well, the importance of darkness. So, as we celebrate the awakening, the visual delights, and the opportunity to find our way that the morning brings, we also give thanks for the rest, repose, and renewal that are the potential gifts of the night.

PETER WELLER

This flame glows
　　as light glows in the darkness.
This flame dances
　　as growing things dance upon the green earth.
This flame flickers
　　as life flickers for a precious while in each of us.
This flame is warm
　　as the companionship of family and friends is warm.

ANDREW M. HILL

Flaming chalice, burning bright,
now you share with us your light.
May we always learn to share
with all people everywhere.

EVA M. CESKAVA, ADAPTED

We light this candle to remind ourselves to treat all people
  kindly, because they are our brothers and sisters.
We light this candle to remind ourselves to take good care
  of the earth, because it is our home.
We light this candle to remind ourselves to live lives full
  of goodness and love, because that is how we will become
  the best men and women we can be.

ANONYMOUS

We gather this hour as people of faith
With joys and sorrows, gifts and needs.
We light this beacon of hope, sign of our quest
for truth and meaning,
in celebration of the life we share together.

CHRISTINE ROBINSON

We light this chalice to celebrate the love within us, among us, and all around us.

DAVID HERNDON

This Sacred Moment

We light this candle as a symbolic act
to establish a time in our week when rituals have meaning,
stories tell the truth,
and the spirit speaks louder than words
of the transcendent mystery of creation
and our place in the universe.

MARSHALL HAWKINS

As others before us have sought to make ordinary
    times special by lighting a candle,
we now seek to transform this ordinary time
    into a special and sacred one
by lighting the flaming chalice, symbol of our faith.

PENNY HACKETT-EVANS

We see the chalice light.
Let it symbolize today
    the light within.
Let it shine today
    through each one of us,
    in the way we feel
    and in what we do.
Let the light shine.

ROBERT M. DOSS

Loss

When we remember, O God, those we have loved and lost,
help us to remember also how great a thing is loving, and that not
to have loved would have been far greater loss.

A. POWELL DAVIES

In our time of grief, we light a flame of sharing, the flame of ongoing
life. In this time when we search for understanding and serenity in
the face of loss, we light this sign of our quest for truth, meaning,
and harmony.

CHRISTINE ROBINSON

When sorrow comes, let us accept it simply, as a part of life. Let the heart be open to pain; let it be stretched by it. All the evidence we have says that this is the better way. An open heart never grows bitter. Or if it does, it cannot remain so. In the desolate hour, there is an outcry; a clenching of the hands upon emptiness; a burning pain of bereavement; a weary ache of loss. But anguish, like ecstasy, is not forever. There comes a gentleness, a returning quietness, a restoring stillness. This, too, is a door to life. Here, also, is a deepening of meaning—and it can lead to dedication; a going forward to the triumph of the soul, the conquering of the wilderness. And in the process will come a deepening inward knowledge that, in the final reckoning, all is well.

A. POWELL DAVIES

Seasonal and Special Occasions

Child Dedication

We light this chalice in wonder and appreciation for the gifts of childhood, and we dedicate ourselves to the nurture of those gifts, that our children may grow in beauty and in love.

CONNIE STERNBERG

Spring

We light our chalice to remember the sorrow, the loss, and the joy
    that are within this season of the year.
The Passover, that brought freedom from slavery and bondage for
    the Jewish people, continues to bring light into the world.
Palm Sunday, Good Friday, and Easter, that brought joy and the
    triumph of life over death for the Christian people, still bring
    the light of that joy to the world.
The spring equinox, that brings new life bursting forth on the land
    each year, brings lengthened days of sunlight to all life.
Passover for freedom, Easter for life, spring for rebirth.
We light our chalice for all three.

ELIZABETH M. STRONG

We light this chalice as a symbol of our thankfulness.
The chalice reminds us of the sun, the giver of life.
The flame rises up like the power of growth and renewal in the
    springtime.
We give thanks
    for the sun, which lights and warms the earth,
    for the growth and renewal of nature, arising from the earth, and
    for the earth itself.

DAVID J. MILLER

Summer

As we light this chalice, we are glad of summer light that wakes color in the world so early and keeps it up so late.

We are glad of the light of the mind that does not depend upon the time of day, the time of year, or the time of life to enlighten us and to beckon us inward, outward, and onward in exploration of the many realms of being.

We are glad of the light of the heart that accompanies us in our search for companionship in life, for worthy work to do, and for ways to overflow in joy and in deeds of courage and compassion.

Let us rejoice in the many glad meanings of light.

GRETA W. CROSBY

Thanksgiving

For daylight and darkness,
for sunshine and rain,
for the earth and all people,
we offer deep thanksgiving.
We kindle this light in celebration
of the life that we share.

GARY KOWALSKI

May the goodness of the earth continue to sustain us.
May the goodness of friends and family continue to support us.
May the joys of this holiday renew us.

KATHERINE INGLEE

We drink from wells we did not dig.
We have been warmed by fires we did not build.
We light this chalice in thanksgiving
for those who passed their light to us.

ROBERT SCHAIBLY

Christmas

Into the bright circle of life and light, which is the Christmas season, we have come. Out of the routine ways of living, and the drab little ruts of habit, we have come to warm our hearts and minds at the cradle of the child.

May something of the beauty, mystery, and promise of this lovely old story fall like silver rain upon the broken dreams, the hates and fears of all.

Once again may we pause, look up, and in the far-off distances hear that old, old music, the music of hope, brotherhood, sisterhood, and blessed peace!

ALFRED S. COLE

May the candles we light this holiday season remind us of the glowing love within the heart. May the carols we sing uplift our spirits and renew our hope and vision. May the special moments we spend with family and friends strengthen the bonds of caring between us at this time and throughout the coming year.

PATRICK GREEN

Prayers and Meditations

Praise the Blue Sky

I praise the blue sky.
I praise the sun that is in you.
I praise the bright moon.
I praise the shining stars in you.

ANONYMOUS

We give thanks for the earth and its creatures
    and are grateful from A to Z:
For alligators, apricots, acorns, and apple trees,
For bumblebees, bananas, blueberries, and beagles,
Coconuts, crawdads, cornfields, and coffee,
Daisies, elephants, and flying fish,
For groundhogs, glaciers, and grasslands,
Hippos and hazelnuts, icicles and iguanas,

For juniper, jackrabbits, and junebugs,
Kudzu and kangaroos, lightning bugs and licorice,
For mountains and milkweed and mistletoe,
Narwhals and nasturtiums, otters and ocelots,
For peonies and persimmons, and polar bears,
Quahogs and Queen Anne's Lace,
For raspberries and roses,
Salmon and sassafras, tornadoes and tulipwood,
Urchins and valleys and waterfalls,
For X (the unknown, the mystery of it all!)
In every yak and yam;
We are grateful, good Earth, not least of all,
For zinnias, zucchini, and zebras,
And for the alphabet of wonderful things
that are as simple as ABC.

GARY KOWALSKI

I have seen the waters flow in the river.
I have seen the flowers along the banks of the river.
Passing by, I have gazed upon the countryside
        and inhaled the perfume of the orange blossoms.
I have been grateful to God and I have said thank you.

ALGERIAN PRAYER

The earth's so big and I'm so small,
I wonder why I'm here at all,
until, at dark, I see the sky
and then I think I know just why.

I'm here to look and think and ask.
To wonder seems to be my task.
That suits me fine; there's much to see.
I sure am glad on earth to be.

JANET GOODE

Whatever road I take
    joins the highway
    that leads to God.
Broad is the carpet God has spread
    and beautiful are its colors.

PERSIAN SCRIPTURE

Blessed is the spot, and the house, and the place,
and the city, and the heart, and the mountain,
and the refuge, and the cave, and the valley,
and the land, and the sea,
and the island, and the meadow
    where mention of the holy has been made

and praise of the sacred glorified.
Blessed be. Amen.

BAHÁ'U'LLÁH, ADAPTED

Let us pray to the God who holds us in the hollow of His hands, to
    the God who holds us in the curve of Her arms,
to the God whose flesh is the flesh of hills and hummingbirds and
    angleworms,
whose skin is the color of an old black woman and a young white
    man, and the color of the leopard and the grizzly bear and the
    green grass snake,
whose hair is like the aurora borealis, rainbows, nebulae,
    waterfalls, and a spider's web,
whose eyes sometimes shine like the Evening Star, and then like
    fireflies, and then again like an open wound,
whose touch is both the touch of life and the touch of death,
and whose name is everyone's, but mostly mine.
And what shall we pray?
Let us say, "Thank you."

MAX A. COOTS

Great Spirit, whose voice I hear in the winds and whose breath
gives life to the world: as I come before You, one of Your many
children, I am small and weak; I need your strength and wisdom.

May I walk in beauty; may my eyes behold the red and purple sunset; may my hands respect what You have made; may my ears be sharp to hear Your voice.

Make me wise, so I may know what You teach in every leaf and rock.

Make me strong, so I may be able to fight my greatest enemy, myself.

May I ever be ready to come to You with clean hands and straight eyes, so that when life fades like a sunset, I may come to You without shame.

LAKOTA PRAYER

Interdependence

As we sit here quietly, we are aware of our connections with each other in this room; we are aware of our connections with people of faith all around the world; we are aware of our connections with all of nature—in fact, the universe itself. May we truly experience and appreciate our interdependence with all of life.

RODNEY E. THOMPSON

Holy and Creative Light, teach us to love this Earth, our home.

Together we live in one small house, even though to us it seems so large and with so many rooms. This quiet planet, marbled blue and white, was hanging here and spinning in black space long before we came. Whole families, kingdoms, empires of teeming life arose and passed away before us. Now we are here, not knowing how or why.

Slowly we have begun to learn about our house: how delicate, how self-contained, how easily torn apart! Holy it is, this bubble of rock, water, air—not to be consumed nor smashed like the toy of a careless child, but to be cared for and cherished, to be kept clean and liveable for all the later tenants in their generations.

Teach us to be servants of life, not prideful masters. For we are caretakers and stewards here, with this great responsibility: to watch over the house, to savor its beauty, to breathe its air.

CHARLES GRADY

Great Spirit, fill us with light.
Give us the strength to understand and eyes to see.
Teach us to walk the soft earth as relatives to all that live.

SIOUX PRAYER

Hold on to what is good,
　　even if it is a handful of earth.
Hold on to what you believe,
　　even if it is a tree that stands by itself.
Hold on to what you must do,
　　even if it is a long way from here.
Hold on to the hand of your neighbor,
　　even when you are apart.

PUEBLO BLESSING, ADAPTED

Eternal God, Mother and Father, Spirit of Life,
We are grateful for the companionship of hearts and minds seeking
　　to speak the truth in love.
We are grateful for our heritage, for the women and men before us
　　whose prophetic words and deeds make possible our dreams
　　and our insight.
We are grateful for the gift of life itself, mindful that to
　　respect life means both to celebrate what it is and to insist on
　　what it can become.
May we always rejoice in life and work to cultivate a sense of its
　　giftedness, but may we also heed the call to transformation and
　　growth.
May we find in ourselves the strength to face our adversities, the
　　integrity to name them, and the vision to overcome them.

May we honor in pride the heroines and heroes of our past, but
may we also keep company with the fallen, the broken, and the
oppressed, for in the dazzling of noonday's heat, and in the
star-studded shimmering of night's rich blackness, we are them.

M. SUSAN MILNOR

O Spirit of Compassion,
enter our hearts, we pray.
Be with us in the hard hours.
Help us to be kind this day.

O Spirit of Unity,
help us enter into the pain of our neighbors.
Let us walk where they walk,
that we might speak a gentle word along the way.

O Spirit of Love,
enlarge our sympathies toward all troubled folk.
Let us be generous of heart,
that we might forgive and be forgiven.

O Spirit of Thanksgiving,
let us be grateful for hands that serve,
for those who give,
and for those who receive.

O Spirit of Life,
let us walk together in our weakness,
that by treading the path together
we may be made strong.

O Spirit of the Spheres,
help us to face the mystery of being.
Secure us in the larger patterns we can trust,
and bless us this holy day.

RICHARD S. GILBERT

May we have eyes that see, hearts that love,
and hands that are ready to serve,
for we would take our part as good neighbors in this wide world.

JACKIE CREUSER, ADAPTED

O God, whom we know as Love,
help us to recognize the love that surrounds us and in which we
    have our being.
Help us to see ourselves as the loving people we are and can be.
In silence, now, we bring to our mind's eye the people who have
    loved us and continue to love us,
        people who are not here with us today, but whose love we carry
            with us,

people who are there every day, and whose love we sometimes
    take for granted,
people who might be within our circle of love, could we
    but extend it a little further.
In silence, now, we hold these people in our hearts.

(*Silence*)

In returning from silence, we ask that our hearts may be opened to
    all whose names and faces have crossed our minds and that the
    love we share with the people in our lives may be our abiding
    teacher.

WAYNE B. ARNASON

Forgive us that often we forgive ourselves so easily and others so
    hardly;
Forgive us that we expect perfection from those to whom we show
    none;
Forgive us for repelling people by the way we set a good example;
Forgive us the folly of trying to improve a friend;
Forbid that we should use our little idea of goodness as a spear to
    wound those who are different;
Forbid that we should feel superior to others when we are only
    more shielded;
And may we encourage the secret struggle of every person.

VIVIAN POMEROY

The friendship we share this day is sacred.
    All gatherings when people meet and touch,
    celebrate life.
The laughter we share this day is sacred.
    Joy and sorrow that rise from love
    are springs of life.
The stillness we share this day is sacred.
    In this peace is a haven for the spirit
    that nurtures life.
For friends, for joy and sorrow, for the comfort of quietness,
    let us ever be grateful and caring.

RUDOLPH W. NEMSER

O Thou, whose kingdom is within,
may all thy names be hallowed.
May no one of them be turned against the others
to divide those who address thee.

May thy presence be made known to us
in mercy, beauty, love, and justice.
May thy kingdom come to be in the life
of all humankind.
May it come with peace, with sharing,
and in a near time.

Give us this day our daily bread,
free from all envy and alienation,
broken and blessed in the sharing.

Keep us from trespass against others,
and from the feeling that others are
trespassing against us.
Forgive us more than we have forgiven.

Deliver us from being tempted by lesser things
to be heedless of the one great thing:
the gift of thyself in us.

JACOB TRAPP

Stillness

Let us be quiet, without and within.
Let the stillness be in us.
Let the silence hold us.
May we find the deep places of the soul and begin to let go of the
    distractions which plague us.
May we let go of irritation, calm the confusion which inhibits us,
    let go of fear.

The quiet is within us.
The stillness is in us.
The silence will hold us.
There are deep places in the soul.
Here, may we find peace.

HAROLD E. BABCOCK

God of life and beauty:
We pray for the quietness of snowflakes, knowing that love
   is quiet.
We pray for the kindness of small acts, knowing gentleness
   is fragile.
We are grateful to know that thoughtfulness makes no sound,
   that compassion leaves wonderfully beautiful traces
   when we open ourselves to wonder.
May ours be a religion which, like the snowflake, goes
   everywhere in quietness, in love, and with gentle
   regard for that which is true and beautiful,
   in us and about us. Amen.

LUCINDA STEVEN DUNCAN

Words tell us of our thoughts,
silence helps us hear our deeper feelings.

In silence, we sense the rhythmic measures of all life
in the slow repetitive rhythm of our own bodies.

In silence, we feel the ebb and flow of life's breath
as the waves of the larger ocean in which we all live.

In silence, we sense a larger spiritual presence
of which we are all a part.

In silence, we sense the coming and going of human pathways,
knowing we can ask no more than to have reached out to others in
creative and caring ways.

And in this silence, we know it is this human touch that gives the
larger journey its meaning.

EDWIN LYNN

Give me beauty in the inward soul,
and may the outward and the inward me be at one.

SOCRATES

To this quiet place of beauty
we have come from workday things,
pausing for a while and waiting
for the thoughts that quiet brings.

ANONYMOUS

Silence is an abnormal state.

The world is nowhere silent:
the wind calls from the tree tops
and whispers in the beach grass.

The world is nowhere silent:
streams laugh aloud,
waves roar as they fall upon the beach.
Were our ears more finely tuned, we could hear
the crack of granite as boulders are reduced to pebbles,
pebbles to sand,
sand to dust.
Were our ears more finely tuned, we could hear
the grinding of tectonic plates as they collide,
the vibrations in the very heart of the atom.

The world is nowhere silent:
    birds sing and chirp,
    squirrels chatter,
    insects hum and whir.
They fall quiet only briefly at our approach,
a suggestion that silence is a sign of fear.

Is it not strange that even as Gaia
    sings to us,
    calls to us,
    shouts at us,
we seek wisdom in silence?

Is it a measure of our alienation
that we retreat into silence,
withdraw from the chorus,
in order to hear
the endless
eternal
song?

DAVID E. BUMBAUGH

Knowing that we do not always live up to our best expectations of ourselves, let us in quietness seek the good within, which some call the Inner Light, and some "a spark of the divine."

(*Silence*)

Knowing that we live in a society that falls far short of the ideal, let us in quietness resolve to do one thing this week to aid those suffering from want and injustice.

(*Silence*)

Knowing that the earth is our home and that humankind is making it a dirty and even poisonous home, let us in quietness consider how we might be part of making it more healthful for all living things.

(*Silence*)

Knowing that each of us has some sorrow or worry hidden within, let us consider in quietness how we may reach out to one another with our smiles, our handclasps, and our encouraging words.

(*Silence*)

MARYELL CLEARY

Let this house be quiet.
Let our minds be quiet.
Let the quietness of the hills,
the quietness of deep waters,
be also in us:
So quiet that the noise
of passing events and present
anxieties,
of random recollections
and wandering thoughts,
is stilled;
So quiet that the marvelous
stillness is like music;
So quiet that we feel
the very being which is
the life of us all;
So quiet that we are renewed,
we feel at one with all others,
at home in a tabernacle
of stillness;
So quiet that we sense
the ripples of this pool
of quietness and healing
pass through us and out
to the farthest star.

JACOB TRAPP

In an unsettled world, we seek for a few moments to turn away from the noise and confusion of our lives. We seek to enter a stillness, a stillness that resides in the depths of each of us, a stillness that is at the center of all that exists.

For a few moments, let us seek quiet—not the quiet that is the
   absence of noise, for there is always noise.
Rather, it is like the stillness of a friend listening,
   the noontime silence of sunlight on a lake,
   the silence of a new idea, a thought that makes
     the world pause,
   the quiet of growing plants,
   the quiet of a child sleeping,
   the silence that brings rest,
   the silence that brings renewal,
   the silence from which hope and love emerge.

Let us pause for a few moments, to listen for the stillness that rests beneath the confusion and complexities of our lives.

   (Silence)

BRUCE MARSHALL

In quiet that deepens into silence
we move from
the surface of sound and the spoken word
to rest in deeps from which springeth all sound,
as a flower trembling
at the edge of living.
Hear our cry, God of the silence,
and hear our laughter.

Signs and sounds of gratitude
tremble into being
as we labor:
the hammer blow is thanks,
and the knotting of a thread, and
listening expectantly at the edge of sound.

All things are thanks and the giving of thanks.

THEODORE A. WEBB

Ordinary Miracles

Simply to be, and to let things be as they speak wordlessly from the
   mystery of what they are,
simply to say a silent yes to the hillside flowers, to the trees we walk
   under,
to pass from one person to another a morsel of bread, an answering
   yes, this is the simplest, the quietest, of sacraments.

JACOB TRAPP

May we attend to the ordinariness of our days
and remember that they imprint our spirits,
line our eyes,
weary our hearts,
stimulate our memories,
callous our hands,
and make whole our lives.

ELIZABETH TARBOX, ADAPTED

For simple things that are not simple at all
For miracles of the common way. . .
   Sunrise . . . Sunset,
   Seedtime . . . Harvest,
   Hope. . . Joy . . . Ecstasy

For grace that turns
> our intentions into deeds
> our compassion into helpfulness
> our pain into mercy

For Providence that
> sustains and supports our needs

We lift our hearts in thankfulness,
> and pray only to be more aware
> and thus more alive.

GORDON B. MCKEEMAN

Promise

Each of us is an artist
Whose task it is to shape life
Into some semblance of the pattern
He dreams about. The molding
Is not of self alone, but of shared
Tomorrows and times we shall never see.
So let us be about our task.
The materials are very precious
> and perishable.

ARTHUR GRAHAM

Let us reflect for a few moments in silence.

As Unitarian Universalists we believe that each individual is free to determine what is finally good and right and true, and that freedom carries with it the responsibility for each of us honestly and vigorously to seek out life's deeper meanings. So let us remind ourselves that our quest is neither trivial nor inconsequential, but of primary concern, if we are to live well and fully.

Therefore, let us reflect on the ways in which each of us feels called upon to change and grow. And let us resolve that in the days and weeks to come we may live closer to that ideal.

Let us reflect for a few moments in silence upon the possibilities for our lives.

DOUGLAS GALLAGER

Acceptance

I wonder if the river ever despairs of its downward destiny and
    harbors a secret desire to flow up.
I wonder if winter yearns to be summer, or if a flower wishes it
    could bloom out of season.
I wonder if silence would like to shout, or if the sky wants to
    fall down and become the earth.

I wonder if the bird longs to become a rabbit, or if the fish ever
dreams of walking on the land.
I wonder if the mountains envy the valleys, or if snow secretly
covets the warmth of June.
I wonder if the moon complains that it is not the sun, or if the
stars envy the earth.
I wonder if rain prefers a cloudless sky, or if grass tires of
green and hopes for blue.
I wonder if spring really likes growing, or if fall rages against
its colorful dying.
I wonder if the world ever sighs after more than it is—as we do,
as we do.
O Spirit of Life, we struggle against our limitations. Teach us to
accept them.

BURTON D. CARLEY

Loss

Eternal Spirit, whom we call God,
you are our life.
You are the best and the most beautiful in us and beyond us.
Your spirit is in animals, birds, plants, and in people
whom we do not know or who seem very different from us.

All of us share the gift of life.
Help us to remember that life is good.
Help us to know that we don't stop loving people or other living
     things when they are no longer close to us.
Love lasts always.
May we look for ways to love one another, and to love
     all living things. Amen.

LUCINDA STEVEN DUNCAN

Source of all life:
We celebrate life's beauty; we are a part of life's joy.
We know that both life and death are real.
We never would choose to part with one we have loved,
     but whenever there is great love, there is great
     memory, a great understanding that we carry in
     ourselves the best of the life that is gone.
May we show our love and celebrate the life remembered
     in our daily small kindnesses and give thanks for the love
     that we share. Amen.

LUCINDA STEVEN DUNCAN

This sparrow died today,
this feathered creature small.
We lay it in the friendly Earth,
which holds and shelters all.

ANONYMOUS

Please center yourself within for a few moments.
Push aside the persistent issues of day-to-day living.
Be aware of the core, the heart of things within you.

Unveil there the memories of those you have loved who have died,
perhaps in the past year.
Find the joy of those memories and let it flow through you—
even as the pain they evoke springs forth as well.
I invite you to say their names aloud as we all pause
in silent expression of our loss and sorrow.

(*pause*)

Each of us has experienced, physically,
something of the pain that can accompany dying.
It is no easy thing for a body determined by genes and guts
to "give up the ghost."
Each has felt, deep within, the fear of death and of dying.
It is the challenge of being human to feel that chill,

the awareness of self and mortality.
Each knows, deep in the heart, the grief that death leaves behind.
It is impossible to love other people
and not be wrenched cruelly by the loss of that love when they die.

We strive not to escape death's pain,
but to find people with whom to share its sorrow.
In the bosom of our family, in the community of faith,
we are all kin in death—as in life.
We come together to affirm that faith, and to feel that kinship.

We yearn always for wisdom
to escape the fear that accompanies mortality.
May we feel that wisdom grow deeper in us today.
We hunt always for the peace beyond our pain.
May we see more clearly that peace today.
We seek always the strength to grieve our losses well.
May we find that strength renewed today.

Amen.

BRAD GREELEY

Peace

O God, who makes peace and harmony
    in the heavenly spheres,
Help your bewildered humanity understand
    the futility of war and hatred and violence.
How long, O loving God,
    will we continue to kill in Your name?
How long will we refuse to register
    the unalterable fact that
    all human creatures on this earth
    are brothers and sisters?
Help us to understand
    that the search for peace and well-being
    is not weakness nor lack of conviction,
    but rather the only way to ensure continued life
    on this planet upon which You have placed us.
Help us prove ourselves worthy
    of Your creation—
    God of all space
        and time and worlds.

JEWISH PRAYER

I desire neither earthly kingdom
nor even freedom from birth and death.
I desire only the deliverance from grief
    of all those afflicted by misery.
Oh, Lord, lead us from the unreal to the real,
    from darkness to light,
    from death to immortality.
May there be peace in celestial regions.
May there be peace on earth.
May the waters be appeasing.
May herbs be wholesome,
    and may trees and plants bring peace to all.
May all beneficent beings bring peace to us.
May Thy wisdom spread peace all through the world.
May all things be a source of peace to all and to me.
Om Shanti, Shanti, Shanti.

HINDU PRAYER

God, Lord of the universe,
    be merciful and compassionate.
Have mercy upon us and illumine our way,
    our hearts, and our minds in this hour.
God, Lord of all dominion,
    whose hand is all good,
    give our leaders humility, wisdom, and good judgment.

Heal us, our compassionate Lord.
Heal our folly by Your wisdom.
Heal our arrogance by Your forgiving love.
Heal our greed by Your infinite bounty.
Heal our insecurity by Your healing power.
God, guide us to Your ways,
  ways of righteousness and peace.
Bring us peace, O Lord of peace.

MUSLIM PRAYER

Eternal God,
shepherd of every hope,
refuge of every bewildered heart,
  hear our prayer for peace.
Save us from weak resignation to violence.
Teach us that restraint is the
  highest expression of power,
  that thoughtfulness and tenderness
  are marks of the strong.
May we never for a moment forget that all are fed by the same food,
  have children for whom they have the same high hope as do we.
May we not weary in our efforts to fashion out of our failures today
  some great good for all Thy people tomorrow. Amen.

CHRISTIAN PRAYER

crying hearts recall
lives quenched in nuclear flames,
ever, never more

honor the past,
but live today, enjoy life,
loving, not fighting

proclaim the future,
labor for peace in all lands
for love of children

STUDENTS OF THE
NAKAMURA TOMOKO SCHOOL

Great Mystery incarnate in every person and dwelling among us in
the midst of our relationships,
we need your help.

In a world torn by violence and fear, do not let our hearts be
hardened.
Let us embrace those who are in need of our support.
Help us to move beyond seeking justice to seeking a world
governed by grace.
Help us to know what needs to be done—and how to do it.
Where we find suffering, may we bring compassion.

Where we find fear, may we bring courage.
Where we find hate, may we bring love.

DUANE FICKEISEN

Seasonal and Special Occasions

New Year

Eternal Spirit,
God of light and darkness,
at this time of year,
when days are short and nights are long,
as we take stock of life,
as we reflect on success and defeat,
allow us an awareness of how far we have come.
Remind us of friends and family who remain
    steadfast and dear to us.
Remind us to bundle together and keep warm
    within our family/community.
Rejoice with us in our accomplishments
    and mourn with us our losses.

Help us to make workable resolutions and goals,
   knowing that our personal lives touch
   and influence the lives of others.
Give us perspective to make priorities.
Be with us, Eternal Spirit,
   as we render designs and draw blueprints
   for the year to come.
So be it.

JUDITH SMITH-VALLEY

Spring

We are waiting for the sun to show its strength. The winter is too long, and spring seems to trifle with us. The everyday cold has made us tired, our neighbors and children and co-workers tired. We are waiting to rise from the dead.

Who is not ready for the poetry of spring: the forsythia that blooms overnight, the digging, the surprise of the lengthening day?

May we savor the air as it grows warmer and easier to breathe. May we love the earth again, and while we wait once more for the sun to show its strength, may we care for one another.

JANE RZEPKA

O mystery beyond my understanding,
Voice in my heart answering to the earth,
And light of distant stars!
O wonder of the spring, leading the seasons on:
The dewdrops sparkling on the web at sunrise,
And unseen life, moving in depths and shallows of the brook,
Trembling in raindrops at the edge of eaves,
Whisper to me of secrets I would know.
O Power that flows through me and all that is,
Light of stars, pulsating in the atoms in my heart,
Whether you are mind and spirit
Or energy transcending human thought
I cannot know, and yet I feel
That out of pain and sorrow and the toil
Through which creation springs from human hands
A force works toward the victory of life, even through the stars.
Here on the earth winter yields slowly, strikes again, and hard,
And lovely buds, advance guards of the spring, suffer harsh death,
And pity moves the heart.
Yet life keeps pulsing on.
The stars still shine, the sun rises again,
New buds burst forth, and life still presses on.
O mystery!
I lift my eyes in wonder and in awe!

ROBERT T. WESTON

Mother's Day, Father's Day

As we come together, may we find cessation of whatever personal
turmoil accompanies us.
May we seek forgiveness for harsh words uttered, or healing words
left unsaid.
May each of us find strength to endure difficulty;
may we find acceptance of those we may not understand.
And, as this season becomes more glorious with each passing day, may
we be aware of each and every miracle around us, and be glad!
On this day when custom reminds us to remember those who gave
us life and nurtured our early years,
let us give deep thanks for each person, female or male, family or
friend, who loved and guided us to be who we are today.
May we find ways to express that love in words and in the ongoing
integrity of our lives.
And let us be supporters of each other in this uncertain venture that
is our shared life, that our lives may be strengthened and enriched.

POLLY LELAND-MAYER

Earth Day

Dear God of earth and sky,
of polluted streams
and birds that cry,
today we celebrate and remember
    to care for the earth,
    to clear its waters,
    to purify its air,
    and replenish its soil
which feeds us fruitfully.

God of earth and sky,
of singing streams
and birds that fly,
we celebrate and give thanks
today
and all our
tomorrows.

JEAN WITMAN GILPATRICK

Autumn

For the beauty of the autumn,
 brilliant skies,
 pale asters,
 dogwood leaves veined with purple,
 smell of dusty decay not to be found another time,
let us be thankful.

For places of peace and strength,
 sanctuaries of holiness,
 communities of caring,
 times of thought, listening silences,
let us be thankful.

For what we have to be held and shared,
 bread,
 wisdom,
 warmth,
 love mysteriously reaching another being,
let us be thankful.

RUDOLPH W. NEMSER

Thanksgiving

O God, when we thank you for what is given to us and not to others,
let us remember to pray softly, for there will be many who will
overhear.

Let conscience search our gratitude! This bounty did not come
to us because, more than others, we are deserving.

O God of Truth, rebuke us—until the needy multitudes press in
upon our prayers.

These are our sisters and brothers! We are one family.

O God, to whom we bring our gratitude, help us to remember the
many who will overhear!

A. POWELL DAVIES, ADAPTED

Eternal God, source of all created things, we would give substance
to our thankfulness by resolving to make right use of the gifts
we have received from your bounty.

With your gift of the senses we would fashion and preserve a world
of beauty for all.

With your gift of reason we would engage in a responsible search
for truth.

With your gift of compassion we would build a world of justice and
mercy.

And with your gift of Being we would walk together in peace.

Thus, in gratitude, may we become faithful servants of your glorious
ongoing creation.

ROBERT R. WALSH

Winter

Darkness now draws a cloak around us.
Late dawn. Early sundown.
These are the shortest days, the turning of the year, the solstice.

Let us name what we celebrate in the dark and the cold:
    quiet, sleep which is a thread of our connection with the
        hibernating animals
    constellations, traced and rehearsed for centuries by our ancestors
    shelter from the heat, the mirror-glare of crops beneath the sun
    homecomings and memory and winter's wisdom, that even
        eager growth must
    slow—and rest—and wait.
Let us rejoice in the gifts of this season.

LIBBIE D. STODDARD

Across the hill and dell, valley and upland,
Smooth as a blanket across the world,
Softly falling, falling,
Quietly, gently as a mother's kiss
On the face of her sleeping child,
The snow drifts down, touches, settles,
Lies on tree and shrub, on field and woodland,
Like a soft mantle,
Making all things new.
So be my heart this day:
The pain of things done and injuries unmended,
The fears of things unseen and long dreaded,
The ache of failures and mistakes of times past,
The sudden angry passion and the bitter regret,
And strength ebbing away with the inexorable beat of time,
All forgotten, or restored to innocence,
Clothed in gentle purity,
The universal forgiveness which whispers to me,
"Behold, I make all things new!"

ROBERT T. WESTON

Christmas

Gifts that matter have no weight.
They are without substance.
Gifts that matter most are given to us by the Hand of Life
      in grace:
    moonlight on fresh-fallen snow,
    frost delicately etched on a window pane,
    crackling fireside, bright because of who is there,
    aromas of cooked food betokening a family feast,
    reunion of those long separated,
    memories of Christmas past, gone but not forgotten,
    anticipations of the new year yet to be,
    gift-givers whom we love,
    the gift of life itself.
Gifts that matter have no weight.

RICHARD S. GILBERT

Kwanzaa

The season and celebration of Kwanzaa is rooted in the ancient and ongoing African ethical commitment to bring, increase, and sustain good in the world. Based on the first harvest celebrations of ancient Africa, the holiday holds fast to the idea that the promise of our present and the flowering of our future depend on our commitment to the cooperative creation and sharing of good in the world. Indeed, in its principles and practice, Kwanzaa is a reaffirmation of the ancient ancestral teaching of Odu Ifa that we, as human beings, eniyan, are divinely chosen to bring good into the world, and that we must constantly struggle to increase it and not let any good be lost.

MAULANA KARENGA

Readings

The Earth's Flavors

Who can be certain where the self stops and the universe begins?
When we breathe, it is the air from the passing wind that fills our
   lungs.
To our nostrils drifts the fragrance of the woodland flower.
When we taste, it is of the earth's flavors and its saltiness.
When we eat, it is of the field's corn and its wheat.
When we open our eyes, they are filled with sunlight and starlight.
Who can be certain where the self stops and the universe begins?

TODD J. TAYLOR

Out of the nourishment of Earth,
of primal soup and dinosaurs,
of common dust and noble rot,
of particles of suns . . .

Out of the depths of timeless Time,
of ebb and flow, and rise and fall,
of ancient stars and seasoned moons,
of epochs and of ages . . .

Out of the mystery of Why,
of aimless curiosity,
of try and try and try again,
of patience and of chance . . .

Bursts forth the wonder of this Earth,
of life sustained in all its forms,
the tall, the small, the damp, the dry,
the humble, and the bold.

Each has its place and time to bloom,
to take from sun and soil and rain
those precious bits of cosmic coin
so graciously a gift.

And then, in turn, to fade away,
and reimburse our universe,
with all that stellar wealth,
which we but briefly hold.

GREG CHUTE

Dirt.
We fuss and complain about it.
We sweep it out of our homes
and dust it off the furniture.
We wash it out of our clothes
and from the faces of our children.

And yet we are drawn to soil.
Is there anything more satisfying
than the feel of warm mud between your toes?
Is there anything more gratifying
than digging in the dirt—
planting and pruning and weeding
and sometimes even harvesting?
Is there anything more rewarding
than the sight of new green life
breaking through the crust of soil,
reaching toward the sun,
uniting earth and sky in its living form?

We are of the earth.
We grow out of the soil.
We are created
by wind and water moving across rocks
and by generations of living things
giving back to the earth

the elements of their lives.

We are of the earth.
We grow out of the soil,
and in the end we, too,
shall return to the dirt,
to the earth from which we came.

DAVID E. BUMBAUGH

Last night, in the hour just before the dawn, I awoke to hear the familiar "honk" of the wild geese somewhere up there in the murk of the October night. Whether they were on their trek to the southland, I do not know, but the honk awakened within me (as it always does) a sense of wonder, something elemental and deep in the heart of life, calling from the skies. What is it that guides them through the night to their destination? It fascinates me.

We are children of earth also. Is there something in our highest moments that draws us toward our goals? In the realm of the spirit does this call, which urges the wild goose to go southward, also move and impel us onward—this something at the heart of things? This is the wonderment that seizes my heart during the southward flight of birds.

ALFRED S. COLE

Often I have felt that I must praise my world
For what my eyes have seen these many years,
And what my heart has loved.
And often I have tried to start my lines:
    "Dear Earth," I say,
    And then I pause
    To look once more.
    Soon I am bemused
    And far away in wonder.
So I never get beyond "Dear Earth."

MAX A. KAPP

Our UU Values

Each person is important.
Be kind in all you do.
We're free to learn together
and search for what is true.
All people need a voice.
Build a fair and peaceful world.
We care for Earth's lifeboat.

CAROL HOLST

We are always dancing, often delicately and with difficulty, on the twin horns of dilemma. In most instances of human conflict, both horns are in some way true. It is their truth that creates the dance, and it is in this very dance that we are free. Whenever an idea reigns unchallenged by another point of view, there is no freedom because there is no choice.

Thus, conflict is the cost of freedom. If we treasure choice we may also learn to honor conflict and discover it may grant us peace and strength and stature. In devotion to the cause of freedom, disagreement may indeed unite us.

MARGARET A. KEIP

If we must choose between judgment and compassion,
    compassion comes first.
If we must decide between religious intolerance and acceptance,
    acceptance comes first.
If there is a conflict between religious dogma and individual
conscience,
    individual conscience comes first.
If there is a contradiction between a literal and a spiritual
interpretation of scripture,
    spiritual understanding comes first.
If the traditions of our forebears clash with the visions of future
generations,
    visionary new insights come first.

If an exclusive, parochial religion vies with an inclusive, planetary faith,
planetary faith comes first.

RUDOLPH C. GELSEY

We wish for you a storm or two that you may enjoy the calm.
We wish for you tranquility in time of trial.
We wish you a cool breeze on a warm day, and pale white clouds
that you may better appreciate the blueness of the sky.
We wish you darkness that you may see the stars.
We wish you anticipation of high adventure, and we wish you the
courage to avoid battle.
We wish you a sense of wonder—and poetry—and music.
We wish you companionship that you may appreciate solitude.
We wish you a friend who will understand you, and understanding
so that you may have a friend.
We wish you may become all that you wish to be, and more than
you hope that you can be.
We wish you a flower to smell,
A hand to touch
A voice to cheer
A heart to gladden
And we wish you someone to love, as we love you.

ROBERT KAUFMANN

You shall not worship the finite and the conditional as if it were the ultimate.
You shall keep to a rhythm of work and rest in the spirit of the sabbath.
You shall keep your promises.
You shall tell the truth.
You shall try to make amends for the things you break.
You shall honor the people who give and sustain life.
You shall honor the earth.
You shall grant to others the same rights to life, liberty, and property that you claim for yourself.
You shall be kind.

ROBERT R. WALSH

In a world with so much hatred and violence,

*we need a religion that proclaims the inherent worth
and dignity of every person.*

In a world with so much brutality and fear,

*we need a religion that seeks justice, equity,
and compassion in human relations.*

In a world with so many persons abused and neglected,

we need a religion that calls us to accept one another
and encourage one another to spiritual growth.

In a world with so much dogmatism and falsehood,

we need a religion that challenges us to a free
and responsible search for truth and meaning.

In a world with so much tyranny and oppression,

we need a religion that affirms the right of conscience
and the use of the democratic process.

In a world with so much inequality and strife,

we need a religion that strives toward the goal
of world community with peace, liberty, and justice for all.

In a world with so much environmental degradation,

we need a religion that advocates respect for
the interdependent web of all existence of which we are a part.

In a world with so much uncertainty and despair,

we need a religion that teaches our hearts to hope
and our hands to serve.

SCOTT W. ALEXANDER

Some beliefs are like walled gardens. They encourage exclusiveness and the feeling of being especially privileged. Other beliefs are expansive and lead the way into wider and deeper sympathies.

Some beliefs are divisive, separating the saved from the unsaved, friends from enemies. Other beliefs are bonds in a universal humanity, where sincere differences beautify the pattern.

Some beliefs are like blinders, shutting off the power to choose one's own direction. Other beliefs are like gateways opening wide vistas for exploration.

Some beliefs weaken a person's selfhood. They blight the growth of resourcefulness. Other beliefs nurture self-confidence and enrich the feeling of personal worth.

Some beliefs are rigid, like the body of death, impotent in a changing world. Other beliefs are pliable, like the young sapling, ever-growing with the upward thrust of life.

SOPHIA LYON FAHS

Deep in our selves resides the religious impulse.
Out of the passions of our clay it rises. . . .
We have religion when we hold some hope beyond the present,
    some self-respect beyond our failures.
We have religion when our hearts are capable of leaping up at
    beauty, when our nerves are edged by some dream in the heart.
We have religion when we have an abiding gratitude for all that we
    have received.

We have religion when we look upon people with all their failings
and still find in them good; when we look beyond people to the
grandeur in nature and to the purpose in our own heart.
We have religion when we have done all that we can, and then in
confidence entrust ourselves to the life that is larger than
ourselves.

RALPH N. HELVERSON

Promise

Let me tell you a story about my friends Sam and Susan. Sam has
always been interested in the mystical, the supernatural, the para-
normal, and the transcendental. He has keenly pursued reincarna-
tion and spent many hours (or is it lifetimes?) wondering about
the metaphysical. Susan doesn't share Sam's interest in these other-
worldly matters. She's got her feet firmly planted on this earth and
is more concerned with meeting her daily responsibilities of work
and motherhood.

One spring evening, as Sam sat in the rocking chair in his living
room, he repeatedly asked himself the same question. "What is the
meaning of life?" He hoped for some "Aha!" experience, some cosmic
sign. He sat for a long time repeating the question under his breath.

All of a sudden, he heard a booming voice! It came from the kitchen. It was Susan yelling, "Sam, what color should we paint the kitchen?"

It hit Sam like a thunderbolt. His question had been answered. The meaning of life was right there, right then. It was staring him in the face the whole time. Everything that happens is part of the answer. The meaning of life is to participate fully, consciously, and responsibly in every moment we are given.

ALAN GETTIS, ADAPTED

If, on a starlit night,
    with the moon brilliantly shimmering,
We stay inside and do not venture out,
    the evening universe remains
    a part of life we shall not know.

If, on a cloudy day,
    with grayness infusing all
    and rain dancing rivers in the grass,
We stay inside and do not venture out,
    the stormy, threatening energy of
    the universe remains
    a part of life we shall not know.

If, on a frosty morning,
    dreading the chilly air before the sunrise,
We stay inside and do not venture out,
    the awesome cold, quiet, and stillness of
    the dawn universe remains
    a part of life we shall not know.

If, throughout these grace-given days of ours,
    surrounded as we are by green life and
    brown death, hot pink joy, and cold gray
    pain and miracles—always miracles—

If we stay inside ourselves and do not
    venture out,
    then the Fullness of the universe
    shall be unknown to us
And our locked hearts shall never feel
    the rush of worship.

MARNI P. HARMONY

Your gifts—whatever you discover them to be—
    can be used to bless or curse the world.

The mind's power,
    the strength of the hands,

the reaches of the heart,
the gift of speaking, listening, imagining, seeing,

waiting

any of these can serve to feed the hungry,
    bind up wounds,
    welcome the stranger,
    praise what is sacred,
    do the work of justice
      or offer love.

Any of these can draw down the prison door,
    hoard bread,
    abandon the poor,
    obscure what is holy,
    comply with injustice,
      or withhold love.

You must answer this question:
What will you do with your gifts?

Choose to bless the world.

The choice to bless the world
can take you into solitude

to search for the sources
of power and grace;
native wisdom, healing and liberation.

More, the choice will draw you into community,
    the endeavor shared,
    the heritage passed on,
        the companionship of struggle,
    the importance of keeping faith,
    the life of ritual and praise,
        the comfort of human friendship,
           the company of earth,
              its chorus of life
                welcoming you.

None of us alone can save the world.
Together—that is another possibility,
    waiting.

REBECCA PARKER

Here we are:
children at the Big Party,
having our moment in the sun,
our piece of the action,
till our bodies give way
and we are called home.

We're one big, not-always-happy family,
given life and breath by an eternal parent
we dearly long to know.
Now we have our one shot at it,
our one time to be a conscious part
of this ongoing cavalcade.

It's not a free and easy trip.
We have to live with pain as well as pleasure,
temptation as well as promise,
loneliness as well as love,
fear as well as hope.
We have to live inside a coat of skin,
wrapped up in drives difficult to control
and dreams difficult to achieve.

And though we are the guests of honor,
we don't get to set the time of the party or its place,
nor are we consulted about the guest list.

This is our time, and there really is just one question:

What are we going to do with it?

JOHN CORRADO

I am wondrously wrought: partly shaped by my biology, partly shaped by my culture, and partly self-shaped.

I am so wonderfully fashioned that the workings of my self amaze and confuse me.

I know I have the power to choose among many paths, yet most of the time I am on automatic pilot, acting out of little-examined assumptions, values, rituals, myths, appetites, and impulses.

I can meet life in many ways:

I can be tough-minded; I can be tender-hearted.

I can move between activity and quietness.

I can express my uniqueness and individuality, and I can forget myself in commitment to family and community.

I can judge, I can bear witness to the good and evil around me, and I can forgive.

I can analyze, theologize, figure the world out, and I can listen to the still small voice of conscience, intuition, the holy spirit.

All these ways of meeting life, and more, are part of the potential that is me. But I am afraid to move very far or very fast from the ways that have become comfortable.

I seek the self-knowledge that may illuminate new possibilities in life, and I seek the courage to try them.

Most of all I pray for wholeness, for a life in which my many ways of living can be connected and filled with the meaning of holy Creation.

ROBERT R. WALSH

To laugh
>is to risk appearing the fool.

To weep
>is to risk appearing sentimental.

To reach out for another
>is to risk exposing our true self.

To place our ideas, our dreams, before the crowd
>is to risk loss.

To love
>is to risk not being loved in return.

To hope
>is to risk despair.

To try
>is to risk failure.

To live
>is to risk dying.

ANONYMOUS

Two travelers on their way to Japan were standing at the rail of the ship looking out upon the vast open sea. After but a few moments, one of the men turned about and walked away, disappointment written on his countenance. Throughout the day, the man returned to the deck rail and then turned his back upon the scene, each time appearing more disconsolate than before.

Finally the second traveler, who had remained at the rail, felt compelled to ask his fellow traveler what it was that made him so downcast on what was evidently a pleasure trip. The first man replied that he had been told that at this point of the voyage he would be able to see Mt. Fuji rising in the distance. However, the haze over the water was apparently not going to lift, depriving him of a sight that he had so long anticipated.

Taking him by the arm, his shipmate led the man back to the rail of the ship and said quietly, "Look higher." The traveler, raising his eyes above the haze, saw, in all its beauty and majesty, the great mountain peak.

ANNE BOWMAN

I wish for the dull a little understanding, and for the understanding a little poetry. I wish a heart for the rich and a little bread for the poor. I wish some love for the lonely and some comfort for the grieved.

I wish companionship for those who must spend their evenings alone. I wish contentment for the aged, who see the days slipping by too quickly, and I wish dreams for the young.

I wish strength for the weak and courage for those who have lost their faith. And I wish we might all be a little kinder to each other.

FRANK SCHULMAN

Loss

Death is not too high a price to pay
for having lived. Mountains never die,
nor do the seas or rocks or endless sky.
Through countless centuries of time, they stay
eternal, deathless. Yet they never live!
If choice there were, I would not hesitate
to choose mortality. Whatever Fate
demanded in return for life I'd give,
for, never to have seen the fertile plains
nor heard the winds nor felt the warm sun on sands
beside the salty sea, nor touched the hands
of those I love—without these, all the gains
of timelessness would not be worth one day
of living and of loving; come what may.

DOROTHY N. MONROE

Peace

Peace means the beginning of a new world. Peace means a whole world like one country. It means that nations are friends; it means joy to the world.

Peace is quiet and calm. It is rest. It is silence after a storm. It is love and friendship. It is the world's dream of dreams.

It means that the strong respect the weak, the great respect the small, the many respect the few. Peace brings comfort and happiness. It brings bread to the hungry. It brings prosperity to nations.

Peace is like a mother to those who have suffered. Peace after war is like sleep after a long journey. It is like spring after winter. It brings sunshine into the world. It is like sweet music after harsh sounds.

STUDENTS OF THE LINCOLN SCHOOL

Seasonal and Special Occasions

For a Special Occasion

When love is felt or fear is known,
when holidays and holy days and such times come,
when anniversaries arrive by calendar or consciousness,
when seasons come, as seasons do, old and known, but somehow new,
when lives are born or people die,
when something sacred's sensed in soil or sky,
mark the time.
Respond with thought or prayer or smile or grief.
Let nothing living, life or leaf, slip between the fingers of the mind,
for all of these are holy things we will not, cannot, find again.

MAX A. COOTS

New Year

A year is gone.
It matters not when it began
For it has ended now.
There were other years,
And some began with a birthday
And some with a death;
Some with one day of the month and some with another.
Some began with a song and others with a lament,
But today I start another year, whatever the month or season;
It is what lies before me that concerns me now.
There will be decisions and tasks;
There will be drudgery, achievement, and defeat;
There will be joy and grief.
All the raw stuff of experience
Waiting for me to shape, to fashion as I will,
And it will never become just what I planned.
However it may appear to others
I can turn it to knowledge and wisdom
Or folly.
If it be hard, I can make of it strength:
It may become bone, sinew, and steel
Or ashes and waste.

Someone might say, "It all depends on what the year may bring,"
But what I make of it depends on me.

ROBERT T. WESTON

I knew a man who had printed on his stationery this proverb: "Nothing is settled. Everything matters." It established a certain ambience for reading his letters, as if to say: what you are about to read is to be taken seriously, but is not final.

I remember him and his proverb sometimes, especially when it seems impossible to change the world or myself in any significant way. Times like the beginnings of new years.

"Sorry, Jim," I say. "It's not true that nothing is settled. In the past year choices have been made, losses have been suffered, there has been growth and decay, there have been commitments and betrayals. None of that can be undone. A year ago no one knew whether during this year one person would become pregnant, another would get cancer, another would take a new job, another would have an accident, but now it is settled.

"One day this year I was present just when someone needed me; another day I was busy doing something else when I was needed. One day I said something to a friend that injured our relationship; another day I said something that enabled a person to see life in a new way. The best and the worst of those days is now written. All my tears, of joy or sorrow, cannot erase it."

If I stay with my meditation long enough, the reply comes. "Robbie," says Jim, "You have misunderstood the proverb. It is true that you cannot escape the consequences of your actions or the chances of the world. But what is not settled is how the story turns out. What is not settled is what the meaning of your life will be."

The meaning of a life is not contained within one act, or one day, or one year. As long as you are alive the story of your life is still being told, and the meaning is still open. As long as there is life in the world, the story of the world is still being told. What is done is done, but *nothing is settled.*

And if nothing is settled, then *everything matters.* Every choice, every act in the new year matters. Every word, every deed is making the meaning of your life and telling the story of the world. Everything matters in the year coming, and, more important, everything matters today.

ROBERT R. WALSH

Spring

Here is a day of promise!
May it be so with me, with everyone!
The gray clouds scudding overhead,
The storm clouds, rain, and the breaking sunshine,
The apple blossoms bursting in pink and white,

The children gleefully running out to splash in puddles,
The grass green, and the buds
Straining into leaves on shrubs and trees,
And the birds singing, joyfully, in the dawn,
Strutting the lawns as proud possessors.
Everywhere life, life bursting through all fetters,
And the heart singing, protesting against gloom,
Shouting its defiance of clouds and cold;
The gay heart exulting in storm and sunshine alike.
This is a day that aches with the promise of life,
Life which will not be denied.
Let all hearts swell with glad acceptance,
Joyful with the sense of the always becoming,
For out of earth, into the air and sunshine, out of ourselves,
There rises spirit in us,
Neither dark nor threat shall thrust it down.
It rises irresistible in us.
This is the season's gift.

ROBERT T. WESTON

They died last year.
We saw their bodies—
brown, dry stalks,
beaten down,
doubled over,

disgracing the garden,
demanding burial.

A long, cold winter.
Snow buried them
in a pauper's grave.
No marker.
Dead.
Gone.
But not forgotten.

March.
The earth stirs.
Green shoots, tender bulbs.
Straight.
Strong.
Sturdy.
Born again.

Grace flourishes.
Miracles abound.
Resurrections are all around us.

PHYLLIS L. HUBBELL

Easter

Jesus is risen from the dead.

The centuries have not been able to bury him.

Forsaken by friends,
sentenced to die with thieves,
his mangled body buried in a borrowed tomb,
he has risen to command
the hearts of millions, and
to haunt our hate-filled world
with the restlessness of undying hopes.

The years bring him increasingly to life.
The imperial forces that tried to destroy him
have long ago destroyed themselves.
Those who passed judgment upon him
are remembered only because of him.

Military might and political tyranny
still stalk the earth;
they too shall perish,
while the majesty of the carpenter-prophet

bearing his cross to the hill
will remain to rebuke the ways of violence.

Autumn

You can't
put the seed back
after the pod has burst.
A featherweight traveler,
the seed knows
how to fly.

On the edge of this little woods
I have seen the milkweed travel,
the one at the bend in the path
appearing across the ravine
after the snows have gone.

It might have been called a Miracle,
the plant that walks,
but for the rites of fall,
like holy days
returning every year

to reveal this mystery:
pods splitting open
and the shiny, silken seeds
glistening in the sunlit air,
taking flight in the wind,
and doing exactly
what they were meant to do.

Seeds know how to fly,
and plants travel
despite their roots.
Miracles happen all the time.
When we have learned this
there will be no turning back,
the journey having just begun.

KAREN HERING

Now is the time to live; now is the time,
As nature may disclose, to savor life:
To know its streams, its woodland hills to climb,
To read its cliffs, engraved with ancient lore,
To share its moods, the carefree and sublime,
And thrill with beauty from its ancient store.

Now is the time, in wonder to explore
From whisp'ring tree and softly answering dove
To storied shells beside the storm-swept shore,
From starflower to the galaxies above:
Then shall peace flood the restless heart once more
As autumn beauty fills the woods we love.

Now is the time to live, to look, to see,
To taste that life is good, to share its zest
And know its patience in the dormant tree,
The budding earth, the motion that is rest;
Creation in each moment flowing free
Nor dread the sunset in the dark'ning west.

ROBERT T. WESTON

Winter

I cannot keep still in summer.
There is too much noise
and so many smells.
It gets hot and sticky
and irritating sometimes.

But toward the bleak midwinter
even running water slows.

The leaves wither and fall,
revealing hillsides and houses, valleys and trees
too far to see in summer.

And as the winter solstice sounds,
complementary quiet comes. With winter arrives the sound of
    snowflakes falling
and the fumbling footfalls of the fog rolling in.

This is the season where stillness reigns.
Is it the silence of death?
Is it the silence of hibernation?

It is a quiet time—even the birds are still.
Perhaps the earth becomes quiet so that we can better hear
the Spirit of Life, who is always whispering to us.
And so I say, Okay, Spirit of Life—I'm listening now.

DANIEL O'CONNELL

Let us not wish away the winter. It is a season in itself, not simply the way to spring.

When trees rest, growing no leaves, gathering no light, they let in sky and trace themselves delicately against dawns and sunsets.

The clarity and brilliance of the winter sky delight. The loom of fog softens edges, lulls the eyes and ears of the quiet, awakens by risk the unquiet. A low dark sky can snow, emblem of individuality, liberality, and aggregate power. Snow invites to contemplation and to sport.

Winter is a table set with ice and starlight.

Winter dark tends to warm light, fire, and candle; winter cold to hugs and huddles; winter wants to gifts and sharing; winter danger to visions, plans, and common endeavoring—and the zest of narrow escapes; winter tedium to merrymaking.

Let us therefore praise winter, rich in beauty, challenge, and pregnant negatives.

GRETA W. CROSBY

Christmas

For so the children come
and so they have been coming.
Always in the same way they come—
born of the seed of man and woman.

No angels herald their beginnings,
no prophets predict their future courses.
No magi see a star to show where to find the babe that will
    save humankind.

Yet each night a child is born is a holy night.
Parents, sitting beside their children's cribs,
feel glory in the sight of a new life beginning.
They ask, "Where and how will this new life end?
Or will it ever end?"

Each night a child is born is a holy night,
a time for singing,
a time for wondering,
a time for worshipping.

SOPHIA LYON FAHS

They told me that when Jesus was born a star appeared in the heavens above the place where the young child lay.

When I was very young I had no trouble believing wondrous things; I believed in the star.

It was a wonderful miracle, part of a long ago story, foretelling an uncommon life.

They told me a super nova appeared in the heavens in its dying burst of fire.

When I was older and believed in science and reason I believed the story of the star explained.

But I found I was unwilling to give up the star, fitting symbol for the birth of one whose uncommon life has been long remembered.

The star explained became the star understood, for Jesus, for Buddha, for Zarathustra.

Why not a star? Some bright star shines somewhere in the heavens each time a child is born.

Who knows what it may foretell?

Who knows what uncommon life may yet again unfold, if we but give it a chance?

MARGARET K. GOODING

Christmas is more than a date in the calendar.
Christmas is a mood, a sentiment, a symbol.
It is the quickening of the presence of other persons
    into whose lives we have invested a part of our own lives.
It is a memory of other days when into one's path
    a special one appeared to turn an ordinary moment
    or a commonplace event into a hallowed experience.
Christmas is home and hearth, the full, free laughter of children,
    the remembrance of friends, and a moment of peace
    amid the noisy conflicts within and without.
It is a gathering up of the transcendent dreams of the centuries,

signalized in the birth of a child
who became the Prince of Peace.
Christmas is a time when goodwill is reborn, and again made real
in the hopes and hearts of us all.

CLINTON LEE SCOTT

Closing Words

Go Forth with Purpose

Let us go forth into the world
through a door of hope for the future,
remembering these words by Martin Luther:

> Even if I knew that tomorrow
> the world would go to pieces,
> I would still plant my apple tree.

MARJORIE NEWLIN LEAMING

Reminded that we are part and participants of the universe, let us
go forth from the quiet of this hour, encouraged to strive toward
faithfulness to the best in ourselves, in others, and in all of creation.

NORMAN V. NAYLOR

I am only one
But still I am one.
I cannot do everything,
But still I can do something.
And, because I cannot do everything,
I will not refuse to do the
    something that I can do.

EDWARD EVERETT HALE

Worship need not cease.
It can echo in our lives,
in our words, in our deeds,
in our moods,
in our dreams.

Carry it with you wherever you go,
wherever you come.

Be a blessing in your going out
and your coming in.

Amen.

GORDON B. MCKEEMAN

May we never rest until every child of earth in every generation
    is free from all prisons of the mind
    and of the body
    and of the spirit,
until the earth and the hills and the seas shall dance
    and the universe itself resound with the joyful cry:
    Behold! I am!

JOHN CUMMINS

Be ours a religion which, like sunshine, goes everywhere,
    its temple, all space;
    its shrine, the good heart;
    its creed, all truth;
    its ritual, works of love;
    its profession of faith, divine living.

THEODORE PARKER

We receive fragments of holiness, glimpses of eternity,
    brief moments of insight.
Let us gather them up for the precious gifts that they are,
    and, renewed by their grace, move boldly into the unknown.

SARAH YORK

If, here, you have found freedom,
    take it with you into the world.
If you have found comfort,
    go and share it with others.
If you have dreamed dreams,
    help one another, that they may come true!
If you have known love,
    give some back to a bruised and hurting world.
Go in peace.

LAURALYN BELLAMY

Humbly we stand in the face of death.
Confidently we stand with Life.
Our strength is the strength of many.
Indeed, it is the strength of all humanity throughout all time
because we share one fate and a great compassion.

May understanding go with us, and peace, too,
that we may live together in charity, compassion, peace, and joy.
In this spirit let us—individually and together—go forth to live and
to love.

EDWARD SEARL

May the quality of our lives
be our benediction
and a blessing to all whom we touch.

PHILIP R. GILES

May the spirit of truth and love
rule our hearts and minds
and guide us into those ways
that will create love, justice,
and peace on the earth.

RICHARD FEWKES

Be ye lamps unto yourselves; be your own confidence.
Hold to the truth within yourselves as to the only lamp.

BUDDHA

In our lives, may we know the holy meaning—the mystery—that
breaks in at every moment.
May we live at peace with our world and at peace with ourselves,
and may the love of truth guide us in our every day.

MARK MOSHER DEWOLFE

As we leave this community of the spirit,
may we remember the difficult lesson
that each day offers more things than we can do.
May we do what needs to be done,
postpone what does not,
and be at peace with what we can be and do.
Therefore, may we learn to separate
that which matters most
from that which matters least of all.

RICHARD S. GILBERT

Remembering that the universe is so much larger
    than our ability to comprehend,
let us go forth from this time together with the resolve
    to stop trying to reduce the incomprehensible
    to our own petty expectations,
so that wonder, that sense of what is sacred,
    can open up our minds
    and light up our lives.

MARJORIE NEWLIN LEAMING

We have a calling in this world:
    we are called to honor diversity,
    to respect differences with dignity,
    and to challenge those who would forbid it.
We are people of a wide path.
Let us be wide in affection
    and go our way in peace.

JEAN M. RICKARD ROWE

Our time together ends.
In the days before we come together again,
may our actions match our words,
may our thoughts be filled with love,
and may we truly make a difference in a troubled world.

JIM WICKMAN

Do justly this day and all days.
Be of goodwill.
Walk humbly before the mysteries of life
and before that gulf which separates us from the ideals we profess.
Live in peace and praise.
Our day is just beginning.
So be it.

ELLEN JOHNSON-FAY

Love

As we leave this friendly place,
love give light to every face;
may the kindness which we learn
light our hearts till we return.

VINCENT SILLIMAN

I say ours is a story of faith and hope and love. I say it is our need for one another that binds us together, that brings us limping and laughing into relationships and keeps us at it when we otherwise might despair at the fix we are in. I say it is the holy we need, the eternal beyond our comprehension, and one place we can find it is here, working and worshipping together. And I say there is a transcendent value worthy of our loyalty, upon which we may set our hearts, and its divine manifestation is love.

ELIZABETH TARBOX

May the Love that overcomes all differences,
heals all wounds,
puts to flight all fears,
reconciles all who are separated,
be in us and among us, now and always.

FREDERICK E. GILLIS

O Spinner, Weaver, of our lives,
your loom is love.
May we be empowered by that love
to weave new patterns of truth and justice
into a web of life that is strong, beautiful, and everlasting.

BARBARA WELLS

If you have come here seeking God, may God go with you.
If you have come here seeking the way, may a path be found.
If you have come here seeking community, may we be your friends.
If you have come here seeking spiritual renewal, may you leave here
    strengthened in faith,
    renewed in hope,
    and touched by the experience of love.

CHARLES HERRICK

May the patience that makes life tolerable,
    the laughter that eases pain,
    the reverence that makes life holy, and
    the love that is God
be with us now and in every time.

MAX A. COOTS

Let us go forth from this place ready to
  extend a hand to others,
  open our hearts in sharing, and
  find kind words of praise for all we meet.

ALEXANDER MEEK, JR.

Dare we look into one another's eyes
and discover there a friend?
Dare we lower our masks and confess
our humanity is flawed
and still profess
compassion for one another?

In whose spirit do we congregate?
Or why do we bother
to struggle and celebrate
our common life?

Perhaps it is in recognition
of this truth that we sustain:
no matter who we are or why,
we all need a friend along the way.

LAURALYN BELLAMY

Take courage, friends.
    The way is often hard,
    the path is never clear,
    and the stakes are very high.
Take courage, for deep down, there is another truth:
    You are not alone.

WAYNE B. ARNASON

May we follow the path of faith and love this day and in all our days to come.

ALAN G. DEALE

Between the dawn and dark of our being, let us be brave and loving. In our little passage through the light, let us sustain and forward the human venture—in gentleness, in service, and in thought.

CARL SEABURG

Rejoice

With faith to face our challenges,
with love that casts out fear,
with hope to trust tomorrow,
we accept this day as the gift it is:
    a reason for rejoicing.

GARY KOWALSKI

May the peace of flowing water be with us;
may the beauty of starry skies be with us;
may the warmth of companionship be with us;
and may the miracle of this world in its fullness bless us this
    day and each day of our lives.

MARYELL CLEARY

Beauty is before me, and beauty behind me.
Above me and below me hovers the beautiful.
I am surrounded by it; I am immersed in it.
In my youth, I am aware of it,
and, in old age, I shall walk quietly the beautiful trail.
In beauty it is begun. In beauty it is ended.

NAVAJO POEM

May our hearts rejoice in heavenly mirth, being set at liberty, established in gentleness, enduring in charity, surprised by joy.

JOHN F. HAYWARD

Seasonal and Special Occasions

Spring

May the warm sun
shine upon us.
May the brightness of the green grass
fill us with exultation.
May the sweet perfume of the spring flowers
scent the place where we stand.
May the songs of the birds
bring music to our souls,
and love,
fresh and bright,
renew our lives.

ROLAND E. MORIN

May the spirit of life, a gift of the earth's renewal, come awake inside us again. And may we find it holy!

JUDITH E. MEYER

Easter

May we have joy this Easter, a joy born of life well lived;
may we have love this Easter, a love stronger than death,
bringing healing and new growth to our lives;
and may we have peace this Easter, peace that allows us
to be open to the newness of the season
and gives us reason to sing.

JUDITH G. MANNHEIM

Now let us go forth with the faith that life is worth living, that defeat and adversity can be transformed into victory and hope, that love is eternal, and that life is stronger than death.

And may that faith inspire us to live our lives with dignity, love, and courage in the days and weeks ahead.

WILLIAM R. MURRY

Summer

Happiness and summer joys are made of
    peepers breaking the silence of the night,
    mourning doves cooing in the early dawn,
    wildflowers hidden along a forest path,
    and a child presenting a bouquet of dandelions.
It is through such gentle and often quiet nudgings from nature
    that we commune with the sustaining forces of life.
It is through such gentle and quiet communion with family, friends,
    and occasional strangers that we we encounter the divine.

CHARLES J. STEPHENS

Thanksgiving

May we be inspired with gratitude for the wondrous gifts
    that are ours
and be filled with the resolve to share them
    with all who are in need.
May we hold precious one another, and the world
    which provides us with sustenance and beauty.
And may a song of thanksgiving be on our lips to the creator
    and sustainer of life.

MARTA M. FLANAGAN

Christmas

May every one of us know a midnight clear,
 a midnight and a dawn and daytime when we know our desert
 and know the shape of our journey.
May we hear the love songs sung by all good angels
 and learn to sing them wherever our lives take us.
May peace be the spirit of our hearts
 and the work of our hands.
And may joy and hope ever accompany our footsteps.
Amen.

LIBBIE D. STODDARD

Let us sing the song of angels now, the song of hope, of love, of
 courage, of everlasting exaltation.
May our ears always be open to the voice of angels, to the song of the
 spirit, to the solemnity of solitude.
May our voices never fear to sing out in praise of the birth of new life,
 new hope, and a new future.
So be it.

MICHAEL A. MCGEE

May the love of this season be with us through all the days of the year and give us strength and courage and faith. May the peace of this season be ever in us and bring us comfort and hope. May the light of this season shine in our hearts and bring us happiness and laughter. May the joy that is in us be shared with others.

KENNETH W. PHIFER

Christmas is for everyone. Christmas touches the child within and awakens us to the joys of times past. Let us also celebrate the present and build memories for the future. Let us go forth with joy.

ROBERTA M. NELSON

Table Graces

For the food we will receive,
     let us be thankful.
For the people, land, animals, and plants that have made this food
    possible,
     let us be thankful.
For all those who share this food with us,
     let us be thankful.
May receiving these gifts inspire us to share our gifts with the people
    of the earth.
     Amen.

GINGER LUKE

For all we eat, for all we wear,
for all good things everywhere,
we thank you, God. Amen.

ANONYMOUS

Earth, who gives to us this food,
Sun, who makes it ripe and good:
Dear Earth, dear Sun, by you we live;
to you our loving thanks we give.

ANONYMOUS

May we have grateful hearts, and may we be mindful of the needs
of others. Amen.

ANONYMOUS

God, we thank you for this food,
for rest and home and all things good,
for wind and rain and sun above,
but most of all, for those we love.

ANONYMOUS

For health and strength and daily food, we give you thanks,
O God. Amen.

ANONYMOUS

Here at the table now we pray:
    keep us together day by day;
    may this, our family circle, be
    held fast by love and unity.

JOHN S. MACKEY

In the light of love and the warmth of this family
we gather to seek, to sustain, and to share. Amen.

ANONYMOUS

A circle of friends is a blessed thing.
Sweet is the breaking of bread with friends.
For the honor of their presence at our table
    we are deeply grateful. Amen.

ANONYMOUS

We lift our hearts in thanks today
for all the gifts of life.

PERCIVAL CHUBB

The food that we are about to eat
    is the fruit of the labor of many beings and creatures.
We are grateful for it and bless it.
May it give us strength, health, and joy,
    and may it increase our love as a family/for each other/for the
    human family.

JOHN R. B. SZALA

For bread, for friends, for joy and sorrow, for the comfort of quietness,
let us ever be grateful and caring.

RUDOLPH W. NEMSER

> May we hold hands quietly for a moment,
> feeling love flow around us and through us,
> knowing that as we give love away
> there is always more within.

ANONYMOUS

Bedtime Prayers

I am thankful for the night
and for the pleasant morning light,
for health and strength and loving care
and all that makes the world so fair. Amen.

ANONYMOUS

Give me, O God, your blessing
before I give myself to sleep;
and while I slumber,
watch over all those I love. Amen.

COLOMBIAN PRAYER

Thank you, God, for all life brings,
for health and play and all good things,
and help me use my heart and mind
to make me strong and keep me kind. Amen.

ROBERT AND POLLY COOPER

Credits

Readings appear on page numbers in parentheses.

ALEXANDER   *Salted with Fire* (90) by Scott Alexander, 1994. Used with permission of author (16, 90).

ALGERIAN PRAYER   Selection (42), in *UNICEF Book of Children's Prayers*, edited by William I. Kaufman. Copyright © 1970 by William I. Kaufman. Used with permission of William I. Kaufman.

ANONYMOUS   Source unknown (5, 33, 41, 55, 66, 100, 137, 138, 139, 140, 141).

ARNASON   Selection (129) by Wayne Arnason, published in different form in *Singing the Living Tradition*, 1993. Used with permission of author (13, 29, 49, 129).

BABCOCK   Used with permission of Harold E. Babcock (31, 52).

BACKUS   Used with permission of Andrew Backus (2).

BAHÁ'U'LLÁH   Selection (43) adapted from Bahá'u'lláh, in *Baha'i Prayers*, 1985.

BATES   Used with permission of Lindsay Bates (16, 28).

BELL   Used with permission of Jeanne H. M. Bell (23).

BELLAMY   "Invocation in the Spirit of Christmas" (22) by Lauralyn Bellamy. Selection (122) by Lauralyn Bellamy, published in different form in *Singing the Living Tradition*, 1993. "A Friend Along the Way" (128) by Lauralyn Bellamy. Used with permission of author.

BELLETINI   Selection (9) by Mark Belletini, in *First Days Record*, November 1995. Used with permission of author.

BOWMAN   Selection (100) adapted from "Look Higher" by Anne Bowman, in *To Meet the Asking Years*, edited by Gordon B. McKeeman, 1984. Used with permission of author.

BREWER   Used with permission of James C. Brewer (1).

BROOKS   Used with permission of George G. Brooks (7).

BUDDHA   Selection (123) by Gautama Buddha, translator unknown, in *Singing the Living Tradition*, 1993.

BUMBAUGH   "Meditation on Silence" (55) by David E. Bumbaugh, in *First Days Record*, October 1999. "Dirt" (85) by David E. Bumbaugh, in *First Days Record*, May 1998. Used with permission of author.

CARLEY   Used with permission of Burton D. Carley (63).

CESKAVA   Selection (33) adapted from Eva M. Ceskava. Used with permission of author.

CHRISTIAN PRAYER   Selection (70) adapted from the National Council of Churches website, www.ncccusa.org.

CHUBB   Selection (23) by Percival Chubb, in *Celebrating Christmas*, edited by Carl Seaburg, 1983. Selection (139) by Percival Chubb, in *Singing the Living Tradition*, 1993. Used with permission of the American Ethical Union, copyright © 1955. The American Ethical Union Library Catalog number 54:11625.

CHUTE   "Borrowing" (83) by Greg Chute, in *First Days Record*, March 1996. Used with permission of author.

CLEARY   Used with permission of Maryell Cleary (14, 21, 57, 130).

COLE   Selection (40) by Alfred S. Cole, in *Celebrating Christmas,* edited by Carl Seaburg, 1983. *Give Me No Finished Chart: Materials for Modern Worship* (86) by Alfred S. Cole, 1968. Used with permission of Unitarian Universalist Historical Society.

COLOMBIAN PRAYER   Selection (141), in *UNICEF Book of Children's Prayers*, edited by William I. Kaufman. Copyright © 1970 by William I. Kaufman. Used with permission of William I. Kaufman.

COOPER   Selection (141) by Robert and Polly Cooper. Used with permission of Polly Cooper.

COOTS   Selection (104) by Max A. Coots, published in different form in *Singing the Living Tradition*, 1993. Used with permission of author (44, 104, 127).

CORRADO   Used with permission of John Corrado (97).

COTTER   Used with permission of Marianne Hachten Cotter (3, 28).

CREUSER   Selection (48) adapted from Jackie Creuser. Used with permission of author.

CROSBY   *Tree and Jubilee* (115) by Greta W. Crosby, 1982. Used with permission of author (38, 115).

CUMMINS   Used with permission of John Cummins (121).

DAME   Used with permission of Calvin O. Dame (5).

DAVIES   *The Language of the Heart* (35, 78) by A. Powell Davies, 1956. *The Faith of an Unrepentant Liberal Heart* (36) by A. Powell Davies, 1947. Used with permission of Muriel Davies.

DAY   Used with permission of Frances Reece Day (1).

DEALE   Used with permission of Alan G. Deale (28, 129).

DEWOLFE   Selection (123) by Mark Mosher DeWolfe. Used with permission of James Moore.

DOSS   Used with permission of Robert M. Doss (35).

DOTY   Used with permission of Bettye A. Doty (32).

DUNCAN   Used with permission of Lucinda Steven Duncan (53, 64, 65).

FAHS   Selections (10, 12) by Sophia Lyon Fahs, sources unknown. "It Matters What We Believe" (92) and selection (115) by Sophia Lyon Fahs, published in different form in *Singing the Living Tradition,* 1993.

FARBER-ROBERTSON   Used with permission of Anita Farber-Robertson (7).

FEWKES   "Journey Into Oneness" (11), in *Blessed Be* by Richard Fewkes, 1994. *The Heart and Mind's Delight* (123) by Richard Fewkes, 1984. Used with permission of author.

FICKEISEN   Selection (71) by Duane Fickeisen, in *Quest*, February 2003. Used with permission of author.

FLANAGAN   Used with permission of Marta M. Flanagan (7, 11, 133).

GALLAGER   Used with permission of Douglas Gallager (63).

GELSEY   Selection (93) by Rudolph C. Gelsey, in *First Days Record*, January 1992. Used with permission of author.

GETTIS   Selection (98) adapted from "The Meaning of Life," in *Seven Times Down, Eight Times Up: Landing on Your Feet in an Upside Down World* by Alan Gettis, 2004. Used with permission of author.

GILBERT   Used with permission of Richard S. Gilbert (18, 48, 81, 124).

GILES   Used with permission of Philip R. Giles (29, 123).

GILLIS   Selection (126) by Frederick E. Gillis, published in different form in *Singing the Living Tradition*, 1993. Used with permission of author.

GILPATRICK   Used with permission of Jean Witman Gilpatrick (76).

GOODE   Used with permission of Janet Goode (27, 43).

GOODING   "Why Not a Star?" (116) by Margaret K. Gooding, published in different form in *Singing the Living Tradition*, 1993. Used with permission of author.

GRADY   Used with permission of Charles Grady (46).

GRAHAM   "Meditation" (62) by Arthur Graham, in *73 Voices*, edited by Christopher Raible and Edward Darling, 1971. Used with permission of author.

GREELEY   Used with permission of Brad Greeley (66).

GREEN   Selection (40) by Patrick Green, in *Celebrating Christmas*, edited by Carl Seaburg, 1983. Used with permission of author.

HACKETT-EVANS   Used with permission of Penny Hackett-Evans (34).

HALE   Selection by Edward Everett Hale (120), in *Singing the Living Tradition*, 1993.

HALEY   "Amid All the Noise" (13) by Timothy D. Haley. Used with permission of author.

HARMONY   Selection (94) by Marni P. Harmony, in *Exaltation*, compiled by David B. Parke, 1987. Used with permission of author.

HAWKINS   Used with permission of Marshall Hawkins (34).

HAYWARD   "A Benediction" (131) by John F. Hayward, in *73 Voices*, edited by Christopher Raible and Edward Darling, 1971. Used with permission of author.

HELVERSON   "Impassioned Clay" (92) by Ralph N. Helverson, published in different form in *Singing the Living Tradition*, 1993. Used with permission of author.

HERING   "Seeds Know How to Fly" (111) by Karen Hering, in *Creative Transformation*, vol. 13, no. 1, Winter 2004. Used with permission of author.

HERNDON   Used with permission of David Herndon (34).

HERRICK   Used with permission of Charles Herrick (127).

HILL   Used with permission of Andrew M. Hill (32).

HINDU PRAYER   Selection (69), adapted from the National Council of Churches website, www.ncccusa.org.

HOLST   Selection (87), adapted by Carol Holst and the Unitarian Universalist Church of the Verdugo Hills, California, from the seven Principles of the Unitarian Universalist Association of Congregations. Used with permission of Carol Holst.

HOWE   Selection (25), adapted by Charles Howe from a unison affirmation by Napoleon Lovely. Used with permission of Charles Howe.

HUBBELL   "Spring Song" (108) by Phyllis L. Hubbell, in *First Days Record*, March 1997. Used with permission of author.

INGLEE   Used with permission of Katherine Inglee (39).

JEWISH PRAYER   Selection (68), adapted from the National Council of Churches website, www.ncccusa.org.

JOHNSON-FAY   Used with permission of Ellen Johnson-Fay (125).

JONES   Used with permission of Elizabeth Selle Jones (30).

KAPP   "Dear Earth" (87), in *Dear Earth* by Max A. Kapp, 1977. Used with permission of author.

KARENGA   "The Founder's Annual Kwanzaa Message" (81) by Maulana Karenga, on *Kwanzaa: A Celebration of Family, Community and Culture,* www.officialkwanzaawebsite.org.

KAUFMANN   "To Our Children" (89) by Robert Kaufmann. Used with permission of author.

KEIP   Used with permission of Margaret A. Keip (88).

KILLORAN   Used with permission of M. Maureen Killoran (26).

KOWALSKI   "Earth Day" (41), in *Green Mountain Spring and Other Leaps of Faith* by Gary Kowalski, 1997. Used with permission of author (31, 39, 41, 130).

LAKOTA PRAYER   Selection (44) translated by Chief Yellow Lark, source unknown, 1887.

LEAMING   Used with permission of Marjorie Newlin Leaming (119, 124).

LELAND-MAYER   Used with permission of Polly Leland-Mayer (20, 75).

LUKE   "Thanksgiving Grace" (137) by Ginger Luke. Used with permission of author.

LYNN   Used with permission of Edwin Lynn (31, 54).

MACKEY   Used with permission of John S. Mackey (139).

MANNHEIM   Used with permission of Judith G. Mannheim (132).

MARSHALL   Used with permission of Bruce Marshall (6, 59).

MAULDIN   Used with permission of Jane Ellen Mauldin (13).

MCGEE   Used with permission of Michael A. McGee (134).

MCKEEMAN   "For All Occasions" (61), in *Out of the Ordinary* by Gordon B. McKeeman, 2000. "Benediction" (120) by Gordon B. McKeeman, in *First Days Record*, May 1998. Used with permission of author (14, 61, 120).

MCMASTER   Used with permission of Elizabeth McMaster (29).

MEEK   Used with permission of Alexander Meek, Jr. (128).

MEYER   Selection (132), by Judith E. Meyer, in *First Days Record*, October 1992. Used with permission of author.

MEYER   Used with permission of Suzanne Meyer (8).

MILLER   Used with permission of David J. Miller (38).

MILNOR   Used with permission of M. Susan Milnor (19, 47).

MONROE   "The Cost" (102), in *Stopping Places* by Dorothy N. Monroe, 1974.

MOORE   Used with permission of Mary Ann Moore (27).

MORIN   Selection (131) adapted from Roland E. Morin, in *Quest,* April 2003. Used with permission of Mrs. Roland Morin.

MURRY   Used with permission of William R. Murry (4, 132).

MUSLIM PRAYER   Selection (69) adapted from the National Council of Churches website, www.ncccusa.org.

NASEMANN   Used with permission of Raymond R. Nasemann (3).

NAVAJO POEM   Selection (130), published in different form in *Singing the Living Tradition*, 1993.

NAYLOR   Used with permission of Norman V. Naylor (30, 119).

NELSON   Used with permission of Roberta M. Nelson (135).

NEMSER   "The Bread We Share" (140) by Rudolph W. Nemser, published in different form in *Singing the Living Tradition*, 1993. Used with permission of author (51, 77, 140).

O'CONNELL   "Winter" (113) by Daniel O'Connell, in *First Days Record*, January 1998. Used with permission of author.

PARKER   "Your Gifts" (95) by Rebecca Parker, in 1992-1993 course catalog of Starr King School for the Ministry. Used with permission of author.

PARKER   Selection (121) by Theodore Parker, published in different form in *Singing the Living Tradition*, 1993.

PEART   Used with permission of Ann Peart (11).

PERSIAN SCRIPTURE   Selection (43), in *The Humble Approach: Scientists Discover God* by John M. Templeton, 1998.

PHIFER   Selection (135) adapted from Kenneth W. Phifer, in *Celebrating Christmas,* edited by Carl Seaburg, 1983. Used with permission of author.

POMEROY   Selection (50) by Vivian Pomeroy, published in different form in *Singing the Living Tradition*, 1993.

PUEBLO BLESSING   Selection (47) adapted from Pueblo blessing, source unknown.

PUEBLO SONG   Source unknown (4).

ROBINSON   Selection (35) by Christine C. Robinson, in *Singing the Living Tradition*, 1993. Used with permission of author (33, 35).

ROWE   Used with permission of Jean M. Rickard Rowe (125).

RZEPKA   Used with permission of Jane Rzepka (73).

SCHAIBLY   Used with permission of Robert Schaibly (39).

SCHULMAN   Selection (101) by Frank Schulman, in *73 Voices*, edited by Christopher Raible and Edward Darling, 1971. Used with permission of author.

SCOTT   *Promise of Spring* (110) by Clinton Lee Scott, 1976. Selection (117) by Clinton Lee Scott, in *Celebrating Christmas*, edited by Carl Seaburg, 1983. Used with permission of Peter Lee Scott.

SEABURG   Used with permission of Carl Seaburg (5, 129).

SEARL   *In Memoriam* (122) by Edward Searl, 2000. Used with permission of author.

SILLIMAN   Selection (126) by Vincent Silliman, in *Singing the Living Tradition*, 1993. Used with permission of Elizabeth P. Silliman (14, 126).

SIOUX PRAYER   Source unknown (46).

SKWIRE   Used with permission of Marjorie C. Skwire (6).

SMITH-VALLEY   Used with permission of Judith Smith-Valley (72).

SOCRATES   *Phaedrus* (54) by Socrates.

STEPHENS   Used with permission of Charles J. Stephens (133).

STERNBERG   Used with permission of Connie Sternberg (21, 37).

STEVENS   Used with permission of Elizabeth B. Stevens (30).

STODDARD   "Winter" (79) by Libbie Stoddard, in *First Days Record*, November 1995. "Christmas Eve" (134) by Libbie Stoddard, in *First Days Record*, December 1995. Used with permission of author.

STRONG   Used with permission of Elizabeth M. Strong (37).

STUDENTS OF THE NAKAMURA TOMOKO SCHOOL   Used with permission of Earl Anderson. The Nakamura Tomoko School is located in Nagasaki, Japan (71).

STUDENTS OF THE LINCOLN SCHOOL Selection (103), in *Creative Expression* by Gertrude Hartman and Ann Schumacher, 1932. The Lincoln School is located in New York, New York.

SZALA   Used with permission of John R. B. Szala (140).

TARBOX   Selection (61) adapted from "Nostalgia on the 5:42" and "A Story of Faith" (126), in *Evening Tide* by Elizabeth Tarbox, 1998. Used with permission of Sarah Tarbox.

TAYLOR   Used with permission of Todd J. Taylor (83).

THOMPSON   Used with permission of Rodney E. Thompson (45).

TRACY   Used with permission of Denise D. Tracy (26).

TRAPP   Selection (51) adapted by Jacob Trapp from the Lord's Prayer. "In Stillness Renewed" (58), in *In Stillness Renewed* by Jacob Trapp, date unknown. "Simplicity" (61), in *Dawn to Dusk* by Jacob Trapp, 1986. Used with permission of Helen Trapp.

WALSH   "A Nonalogue for the Fridge" (90), "A Man's Prayer" (99), and "It Matters" (106), in *Noisy Stones* by Robert R. Walsh, 1992. Used with permission of author (78, 90, 99, 106).

WEBB   "Giving Thanks" (60) by Theodore A. Webb, in *73 Voices*, edited by Christopher Raible and Edward Darling, 1971. Used with permission of author.

WELLER   Used with permission of Peter Weller (32).

WELLS   Selection (127) by Barbara Wells, published in different form in *Singing the Living Tradition*, 1993. Used with permission of Barbara Wells.

WESTON   "O Mystery!" (74), "A Year Begins Today" (104), "Day of Promise" (107), and "Epilogue" (112), in *Seasons of the Soul* by Robert T. Weston, 1963. "The Snow Drifts Down" (80) by Robert T. Weston, in *Celebrating Christmas*, edited by Carl Seaburg, 1983. Used with permission of Richard Weston-Jones.

WICKMAN   Used with permission of Jim Wickman (13, 125).

WOODEN   Used with permission of W. Frederick Wooden (18, 20).

YORK   Selection (121) by Sarah York, published in different form in *Singing the Living Tradition*, 1993. Used with permission of author.